SMALL GROUP

H E L P

GUIDES

Why didn't you warn me?

by
Pat J. Sikora

Standard®
P U B L I S H I N G
Bringing The Word to Life

Cincinnati, Ohio

Why Didn't You Warn Me?
Published by Standard Publishing,
Cincinnati, Ohio
www.standardpub.com

© 2007 by Pat J. Sikora

Produced by Susan Lingo Books™

14 13 12 11 10 09 08 07   9 8 7 6 5 4 3 2 1
978-0-7847-2075-2

DEDICATION

*I am indebted to many people
for the creation of this book.*

*My husband, Bob, for his
untiring support.*

*Michael Mack, my editor,
who has championed this
work and has labored to
bring this series to
publication.*

*My critique group, which
has honed every word and
sentence. Thanks to Cathy
Armstrong, Judy Squier,
Barbara Milligan, Kathi Lipp,
Kathie Williams, and Katie
Vorreiter for never allowing
me to write less than my best.*

Contents

Getting 1 Started

SEVEN PRINCIPLES FOR GROUP LEADERS

Congratulations! If you're leading a small group, you've begun an exciting adventure. Whether it's a Bible study, recovery group, cell group, or task-oriented group, you'll find that your efforts are richly rewarded in many ways.

First, you'll see people grow in ways that don't happen anywhere else. I've repeatedly been amazed in my years of leading small groups to see people who almost everyone had written off as hopeless come alive and blossom in a group. Throughout this book I'll tell you story after story of people whose lives have been changed through the ministry of small groups.

Second, you'll change. You may think you're leading this group so that the participants will grow spiritually and emotionally. And they will. But the good news is that you will grow at least as much as they will. In fact, it's been my experience that the leader always gains the most from the group experience.

REMEMBER...

"The one who calls you is faithful and he will do it" (1 Thessalonians 5:24)

If God has called you to this ministry of leadership, then you can be sure he will also guide you, equip you, walk beside you, and work through you to accomplish it. Knowing this makes leading a small group considerably less threatening. As you develop your leadership skills through serving, you'll find that leading your small group can be more than rewarding. It can be exciting.

However, it wouldn't be fair to leave you here. Lest you think it's simple, we need to discuss some challenges that can occur in groups. In fact, you're sure to encounter at least one of these challenging people in each group you lead. Rest in the confidence, however, that these are opportunities designed by God and are orchestrated for your growth and the growth of all your group members. This book will warn you of some potential challenges and then encourage you with some pointers for handling them. If the difficulties don't catch you off guard, you'll be able to take them in stride and continue to enjoy leading your small group.

Why Didn't You Warn Me? looks at some of the most common issues that might cause you concern. I'll introduce you to a challenging person and then discuss various ways to deal with the problem he or she presents. Obviously, these are not hard-and-fast rules, but rather suggestions that apply principles of good leadership. You'll need to adapt them to fit your personality, your leadership style, the person involved, and the type of group you're leading. For each challenge, I'll begin with the easiest, least threatening approaches, and then incrementally move to the more difficult, higher-risk recommendations. The good news is that, in most cases, you won't need to progress beyond the first few steps.

START WITH BASIC PRINCIPLES

Before discussing specific challenges, I want to provide you with some general principles of small group leadership that I've found essential in more than thirty years of leading groups. You may find some of these controversial, but they're based on real-life experiences as well as biblical precepts. Behind these principles are stories of real people. I've learned many of these lessons from failure and have corrected them only with many tears and prayers. I hope you'll learn from my mistakes.

Principle 1: The Purpose of Any Small Group Is to Bring Each Member to Maturity in Jesus Christ

> *"Many people grow older, but few grow up."*
> — Familiar Proverb

This principle is the hallmark of any group I lead. I believe that an effective small group can contribute to faster and deeper growth than almost any other type of ministry. I've never been interested in just warming a seat in the church service. I'm not even excited about evangelism in isolation. Yes, it's important to worship and hear the Word taught. And it's vital to share your faith. But in the American church, we have so many Christians who, even after twenty or thirty years in the faith, may grow older but never seem to grow up. They are people who attend church, but don't get involved. People who are won to salvation in Christ, but don't mature.

In Ephesians 4:11-15 the apostle Paul reminds us that the gifts and offices are given to the church to prepare or equip God's people for works of service, so that the whole body of Christ may be built up. The goal is for each one of us to become mature, to the point where we begin to look like Jesus. Note that, contrary to how many Christians live, this maturing process is not optional. Becoming mature is the purpose of every Christian and equipping people for maturity is the purpose of leadership.

Why is this important? Frankly, because many of us are wishy-washy and unstable. Today, as in Paul's day, we live in a world that is full of false teaching, dishonesty, and deceitful schemes. Tolerance is the watchword. Anything goes. Orthodoxy is scorned with, "Whatever you believe is fine. Just don't impose your beliefs on me." In such a society it's easy to be thrown off course. It's easy to lose track of what is an essential of the faith and what isn't. Unfortunately, relying on the Sunday morning service alone won't bring the average churchgoer to the level of maturity required to counter the culture of this world.

That's where the ministry of small groups becomes important. In a small group we not only have the opportunity to hear, but also to study and interact

"It was he who gave some to be apostles, some to be prophets, some to be evangelists, and some to be pastors and teachers, to prepare God's people for works of service, so that the body of Christ may be built up until we all reach unity in the faith and in the knowledge of the Son of God and become mature, attaining to the whole measure of the fullness of Christ.

"Then we will no longer be infants, tossed back and forth by the waves, and blown here and there by every wind of teaching and by the cunning and craftiness of men in their deceitful scheming. Instead, speaking the truth in love, we will in all things grow up into him who is the Head, that is, Christ."

—Ephesians 4:11-15

with God's Word. We have the opportunity to make ourselves accountable to one another for the truths we learn. And we have the opportunity to integrate those truths into the everyday structures of our lives—into our families, our jobs, and our neighborhoods—in very practical and personal ways. We grow in unity with one another, and in the process, we mature. We become adult Christians, capable of discerning truth from error, able to defend our beliefs in public or in private, and willing to stand firm in the heat of trials and even persecution. In a small group, more than almost any other place, we can experience the conclusion that Paul advocates: "Instead, speaking the truth in love, we will in all things grow up into him who is the Head, that is, Christ." This is always my overriding goal as a leader. I hope it's yours as well.

Although I had been raised in a church, I was twenty-eight years old before I heard the gospel. By then I had adopted far too many of the ways of the world. I managed to pull off a professional look on the outside, but inside I was a mess. My insecurities were reflected in skirts that were too short and necklines that were too deep, language that was too coarse and attitudes that were too harsh. My life was meaningless, despite a national reputation in my field. Suicidal thoughts were my constant companions.

God, in his grace, immediately plunked me into a Christian singles group in San Francisco that used a small group approach. Every meeting incorporated the important elements that lead to growth and maturity.

Wise Words

"All of us are to attain to this teleios man of Christlikeness. It does not appear as if Paul [in Ephesians 4:11-16] is giving…Christians…the option of remaining spiritual children. …Whatever Christian maturity is, all Christians are obligated to reach it as quickly as possible, and all Christian leaders are obligated to help those sheep under their influence to reach that point." —Jay Grimstead, *Let's Have a Reformation*

After meeting me, several leaders shook their heads and whispered to one another, "We have a lot of work to do!" But rather than abandoning me to large group settings or ostracizing me because I didn't fit in, they lovingly enfolded me in Bible study, discipleship, and service. They grew me up before I knew what was happening. Because of their excellent equipping, I matured quickly and was then able to do the same for others. That group was a perfect example of the role of the body of Christ in bringing believers to maturity.

Principle 2: People Grow When They Vigorously Interact with the Word of God

The advantage of small groups over the Sunday sermon is that people can interact with the material rather than simply listening to one speaker. I prefer a facilitated discussion rather than a taught lesson because people learn best what they interact with and say out loud.

The problem, of course, is that where there's discussion, there are also challenges. People sitting in an auditorium looking at the backs of heads seldom cause problems for a leader. They don't talk too much or argue or criticize—at least not at the time. They don't go off on rabbit trails or gossip. They just listen and go home. But people sitting in a living room or interacting with others around a table can cause all kinds of challenges. They don't behave like perfect group members, but rather like normal human beings. They bring their weaknesses, wounds, and sins to the group, and intentionally or not, they dump them on the table for the group to fix.

If your group model uses a teaching segment, it's usually most helpful if it's brief and covers primarily background or historical issues. Active discussions that focus on application and accountability are the most effective road to maximum growth.

Note that the operative term here is "the Word of God." Yes, people can grow or learn from fine books written by excellent writers. But they will grow more when the foundation of the study is the Bible itself. This is not to negate the use of a good study guide. Most of us need some direction. Just make sure that the primary object of study is the Word.

"As iron sharpens iron, so one man sharpens another."
—Proverbs 27:17

But it's in their very humanness that they have the chance to grow. The more time members have during the small group time to interact with one another around the Word of God, the more opportunity they have for growth. So when I have a choice, I prefer to maximize the directed discussion time and minimize the teaching time.

Chuck grew up in church and was used to simply sitting in the Sunday service, often

dozing off or daydreaming. He had majored in rough living at college, and he joined the group's Bible study more to have something to do than to really learn. He challenged, usually rather aggressively, everything that was said. He especially fought Bible verses that confronted his worldly lifestyle and standards of purity. However, as the leader and the group modeled a loving adherence to the Word of God and were willing to show him why these passages were important, he softened, matured, changed his lifestyle, and eventually became a leader.

Principle 3: People Grow and Heal Best in Community

Community is, most simply, a place to belong. On the sixth day, God created Adam, but before long he noted, *"It is not good for the man to be alone. I will make a helper suitable for him"* (Genesis 2:18). He created woman, thus forming the first family.

> *"Community is what you were created for. It is God's desire for your life. It is the one indispensable condition for human flourishing."* [1]
> —John Ortberg, *Everybody's Normal Till You Get to Know Them*

Children followed, and since that time, humans have lived in community—in families and communal groupings that provide a place to belong. This was God's plan, his design. Over the thousands of years since creation, mankind has learned that people thrive in healthy communities and languish alone. The family, the church, the town, the club, even Starbucks®—all of these serve the purpose of community.

Sociologists know that beyond the basic economic and structural aspects of community, there is a far deeper purpose for people to interact with one another. In community,

> "[W]e need community...in order to be the kind of people God intended. Without it we are impoverished; without it the human race is in serious difficulty. ... [W]e live in a world that radically undermines precisely the community it so desperately needs. ... [I]t does this by subverting the core ingredients of community—relationships, traditions, and vision. ... [H]umanity requires a healthy community for its general well-being." [2]
> —S. D. Gaede, *Belonging: Our Need for Community in Church and Family*

our strengths and weaknesses are reflected in the eyes of others and as a result, healthy people change and become better. Community helps to shape the individual into that which is valued in the society, whether that society is the family, the church, the town, or the nation. When community works well, these changes are influenced primarily by love and mutual respect. But when community begins to break down, changes are more influenced by coercion and law.

"People need to know who they are. They also need to be reminded who they are, frequently, by those who know them and really love them. And they need repair, so that they can live from the hearts Jesus gave them. That is what it takes to achieve wholeness in a fractured world. It takes belonging to a community." [3]

—James G. Friesen, *Living from the Heart Jesus Gave You*

Ideally, this God-created need for community is fulfilled naturally in family and kinship groups, in villages and small towns. However, in the industrialized world, we've lost the natural groupings and so need to work at deliberately recreating a community in which to be known, loved, and supported. Within the Christian community, small groups are one of the best ways to develop and cultivate deep and meaningful relationships.

In the best of societies, the family, church, and government work together to esteem people and help them grow, mature, and heal. In the worst of societies, these same structures demean people and cause great harm. We see this in our society today where a combination of abuse, neglect, and shifting social values have resulted in many who are wounded beyond measure and can barely function in the community. Increasingly, people no longer know how to conduct themselves in a group, whether that group is a family, classroom, church, or town. Our churches and ministries reap the fruit of this deterioration.

The good news is that God is bringing wounded people into the church for the purpose of healing. Yes, He's doing it on purpose! He's calling the church to form loving communities in which these people can heal. How does this happen?

Wounded people will begin to heal as they are known, accepted, and loved. One church calls this "relational deliverance"—healing through relationships. That won't happen much on the average Sunday morning where most communication is one-way and where it's easy to get lost in the crowd. Rather, it will happen in small groups, social settings, and other places where more mature people embrace the less mature and encourage them to grow. I've seen this happen repeatedly through the ministry of small groups.

Jack had few social skills. His laugh was too loud, and his comments were often "off the wall." He couldn't look you in the eye, and his hugs were tentative at best. As we got to know him, we learned that he was the youngest of several children. By the time he came along, he was generally ignored by his parents and received little in the way of socialization skills. In school, he was at the bottom of the pecking order and developed an inferiority complex big enough to fill a stadium.

> ### WiSe WordS
>
> **"The work of building community is the noblest work a person can do. The desire for community is the deepest hunger a human being can have."** [4]
> —John Ortberg, *Everybody's Normal Till You Get to Know Them*

But beneath his wounding was a love for the Lord and a heart of wisdom. As our group loved him unconditionally, we began to see changes. He knew his problems and was eager to change. He just hadn't known how. Now, with brothers and sisters challenging him in a sanctuary of love, he could learn who God had created him to be and could grow into that person. His laugh became softer and more authentic. He focused better and was able to contribute his wisdom to the group. His hugs became genuine. Within a year, he was invited into leadership in the ministry. Love and acceptance had allowed him to find himself, heal, and mature. That's the ministry of community in small groups.

Principle 4: A Small Group Must Be Small

It's rather obvious, but some people do miss the point: **A small group needs to be small.** That concept is appalling to us Westerners who often measure success by size. We're delighted when our churches or groups grow. We like to boast about how many people we're ministering to. But this fact remains: *to be most effective, a group needs to be small.* The reason is simple: *it's impossible to be intimate with more than a few people.*

To be most effective, a group needs to be small.

Jesus gave us a perfect example. He chose a group of twelve men to walk with him. Yes, he had thousands who followed him and loved to hear him teach. And yes, he gave a significant amount of time to the multitudes. But his closest relationships, his friends, his disciples, numbered only twelve. These men were privy to his innermost thoughts, struggles, prayers, and confidences. He taught them, held them accountable for growth, commissioned them in ministry, and loved them even when they failed.

Caution

Don't give in to the desire to have the most popular small group in the church. Don't think you have to invite everyone who needs to be in a group. Once you grow beyond six to ten members, you'll dilute the effectiveness of your group and compromise the impact the community can have.

Using the biblical model, many small group leaders suggest twelve as an optimum number. For me, it's an absolute maximum. I prefer groups of six to eight members. Why? The main reason is time. If we could spend all day every day together, as Jesus did with his disciples, twelve would be fine. But most of us can't do that. We simply don't have that luxury. We have jobs, families, and other responsibilities. If we're lucky, we get a couple of hours on Tuesday evening together as a group. Therefore, we need a number that is manageable within the context of our lives.

I learned this lesson the hard way one year in a women's ministry. It was an open group, and since I had the largest room, I got all the newcomers. We were delighted that so many women wanted to attend, but it was getting a little...well, messy. Every week we'd run out of time for discussion, prayer requests, prayer, and building community. I knew something had to change. So I deputized one of the more mature members to take on half of the group. They could only move to the other side of the room, but it accomplished the purpose. We got back to a manageable number in each group and the women thrived.

Since then, whenever I lead a ministry where people are allowed to join throughout the year, I identify in advance the leaders who will take on the newcomers, allowing them to form their own small groups as people join. That way, we don't have to split existing groups. This keeps the groups small, while at the same time maintaining the continuity that is essential for maturity.

Principle 5: Minister to the Spirit Rather than the Soul

> **May God himself, the God of peace, sanctify you through and through. May your whole spirit, soul and body be kept blameless at the coming of our Lord Jesus Christ.**
> —1 Thessalonians 5:23

We need to understand that man is a three-part being composed of spirit, soul, and body. Contrary to the usual way we think, the biblical order is spirit first, then soul and body. The spirit of man is that part of him that was created in the image of God and has the God-given authority and responsibility to call the person into behavioral alignment. The spirit, when fed biblical truth watered with love, has the potential to bring healing, restoration, and obedience.

The soul, on the other hand, tends to be a bit unruly. Composed of the mind, will, and emotions, the soul seems to be the defender of the status quo, the defender of "I want to be happy!" The soul is an expert at justifying and rationalizing. Any attempt to talk to the soul of a person about behavior can end up in argument and division, my soul railing against the other person's soul. He then becomes less willing to listen and less willing to change.

But when we speak truth to the spirit, the person is less able to argue. The Word of God, spoken lovingly, graciously, without judgment, and in a community of belonging, is the only thing that has a chance to break through the human defenses.

> *"For the word of God is living and active. Sharper than any double-edged sword, it penetrates even to dividing soul and spirit, joints and marrow; it judges the thoughts and attitudes of the heart."*
> —Hebrews 4:12

So when you face challenging group members, learn to not argue with them. Don't thump them with Bible verses. Simply look them in the eye and speak truth—quietly, gently, lovingly. Affirm their desire to follow God and glorify him. Affirm the image of God imprinted within their spirits. Speak with confidence that you know they know what is right and are the kind of people who will ultimately follow God.

Principle 6: The Group Is More Important Than the Individual

This principle always raises eyebrows. It seems antithetical to the concept of community, but I've learned that it's essential. If it's true that people join a group to grow, they must have a reasonably healthy environment in which to mature. We know that a little leaven can spoil the whole lump. The same is true in small groups. One or two people who bring serious problems *and* (and this is the operative word) who can't or won't respond to leadership or correction will discourage other group members. Soon you'll experience complaining, absences, or both. I've watched groups and ministries deteriorate and shut down because of an imbalance between the more mature and the less mature.

While I always want to continue to minister to these challenging people outside of the group, it isn't wise or fair to sacrifice the growth opportunities of several people to serve one, especially if that one indicates no willingness to cooperate.

**"Don't you know that a little yeast works through the whole batch of dough?"
—1 Corinthians 5:6**

The harsh and heartbreaking reality is that many people in today's society have been severely wounded through abuse or neglect. Others have simply never received the healthy balance of love and discipline they needed as children. As a result, many people today simply can't function in a traditional small group setting—at least as their first group experience. Some are quarrelsome and may or may not be persuaded through excellent leadership. Sadly, others have already developed attitudes of lawlessness, much like the people Paul described in 2 Timothy 3:1-5.

When Paul describes these people who have taken on the culture of the last days and who will not respond to instruction, he doesn't tell Timothy to form a small group and try very hard to change them. No, his remedy is harsh, but essential to protect those in this young church who do want to grow and mature. He says, "Have nothing to do with them."

As we consider the many challenges a group leader can face, very few will require the nuclear option to protect the group. But if you lead for very long, you may have to make the decision to invite someone to leave your group.

Of the people who exhibit the characteristics in 2 Timothy 3:1-5, many want to change and grow. They'll be responsive to the community and the loving leadership described in this book, and you'll delight in the growth you see, slow though it may be. But sadly, a few will not be willing or able to make the changes they need to within the group.

Although I've only faced the need to ask someone to leave the group a few times in more than thirty years, the first time was the hardest because it occurred at the beginning of my very first group. I was still a fairly young Christian and had almost no leadership experience. I was actually the co-leader when

I learned that the leader was engaged in a serious sin. I went to the head of the ministry, and together we had to tell this person that she could no longer be the leader. We invited her to remain in the group for support and accountability, but she refused and quickly disappeared from the ministry and our lives. That was heartbreaking because she had been a good friend, but to protect the group, she had to be removed from leadership. That group, I might add, was one of the most effective I've ever led. I believe God honored our faithfulness to do the right thing, even though it was excruciatingly painful for all involved.

When you have to take the ultimate action of asking a person to leave the group for whatever reason, do so after much prayer and exercising a godly blend of grace, love, and firmness. First, pray for wisdom and discernment. However, by the time you reach this conclusion, you'll have an emotional involvement that may cloud your judgment. You may need to seek advice and counsel from those in authority in the church or from other mature believers. But this needs to be done respectfully, in a way that avoids gossip or talebearing.

It's also true that the stronger and more experienced you become as a leader, the more challenges you can handle effectively. Thus, the decision to ask a person to leave must be a very personal one. You may need help in evaluating when you've reached this point, or if you are honest with yourself, you'll know it.

Caution!
Be absolutely certain that you have no other options before asking a member to leave your group. It is your challenge and privilege as a leader to do everything you can to bring a wayward member into the community for his or her own growth. But in the end, your responsibility is to the group more than to the one.

You will also want to offer alternatives for people whom you must ask to leave the group. While many will simply go away, some will still want to mature and some will be willing to try an alternative setting to grow or heal. Ask God for creative ideas to continue to minister to this one outside of the small group.

I've led groups of profoundly wounded women

TRY THIS CHALLENGE!

This principle issues a challenge to more experienced leaders—those whom God has gifted with tough love and with compassion tempered with firmness. If that's you, ask yourself, *How can I find creative ways to meet the needs of those who don't fit?* Remember that they are still beloved people, created in the image of God, and are never intended to be throwaways.

with the dual goals of teaching them how to be effective group members while at the same time helping them take the next steps toward Christian maturity. I address this concept in Chapter 6. The body of Christ needs

Above all, love each other deeply, because love covers over a multitude of sins.
—1 Peter 4:8

groups like this. We have an obligation before God to help those who want help, to have nothing to do with those who don't want help, and to develop the discernment to know the difference.

Principle 7: Love Covers a Multitude of Challenges

This book deals with challenging people—people who stretch your leadership skills and try your patience. You just want to lead your group and go home. But there's this person who always seems to mess up your wonderful plan. Sometimes when you face challenging people, it's easy to get annoyed. It's easy to just want to be done, to just get it fixed. But please hear this before reading on. These tips for dealing with challenging people are the exceptions, not the rule. The rule is *love*.

You see, if we were to reduce all these challenging people down to the lowest common denominator, we'd find an insatiable need for love and acceptance. We're dealing with people who have experienced a lack of love and acceptance—sometimes a huge lack. And most of them will thrive, grow, and heal in the midst of a community of love and acceptance. Most of our challenging people can be *loved* into community, just as you and I were. I've seen it happen more times than I can count.

WiSe Words

"Everybody's weird. Every one of us—all we like sheep—have habits we can't control, past deeds we can't undo, flaws we can't correct."[5]
—John Ortberg, *Everybody's Normal Till You Get to Know Them*

When people are loved and accepted, they begin awakening like dry plants in rain. These are actions of the heart. They communicate to a wounded person, "I'm glad you're in the world. I'm glad you were born. You have great value in this community."

So don't think that you have to fix everyone before next Tuesday. Use these tips when you need them, but before all else, *put on love.*

The following chapters present many of the challenges I've experienced in leading small groups. Welcome to both the joys and the challenges of small group leadership. May God bless you as you serve him through leading your small group.

ONE FINAL CAUTION!

I've given nicknames to these challenging people just to make them more memorable to you. But please, please, *please* don't put these labels on your group members. Always give them the dignity of being a person, not a label.

[1] John Ortberg, *Everybody's Normal Till You Get to Know Them* (Grand Rapids: Zondervan Publishers, 2003), p. 32.

[2] S. D. Gaede, *Belonging: Our Need for Community in Church and Family* (Grand Rapids: Zondervan Publishers, 1985), pp. 23, 25.

[2] Gaede, p. 35.

[3] James G. Friesen, E. James Wilder, Anne M. Bierling, and Maribeth Poole, *Living from the Heart Jesus Gave You: The Essentials of Christian Living* (Van Nuys, CA: Shepherd's House, 1999), p. 3.

[4] Ortberg, p. 36

[5] Ortberg, p. 16.

Tips for the Leader

2

DEAL WITH YOUR STUFF FIRST

As a leader, you *will* encounter challenges. No doubt about it. But how do *you* make sure that you aren't one of the challenges? Before you can hope to correct problems in your group, make sure that you're following a few simple principles of leadership.

Deal with Your Own Stuff

Let's face it. We all have stuff—unhealed areas in our lives or habits that are unpleasing to God, ourselves, and others. As leaders we don't have to be perfect, but we do have an obligation before God and our group to own, deal with, and heal from our own issues, our stuff. Otherwise, we'll contaminate the group and compromise our leadership.

> **What's It Mean?**
> *Stuff:* a matter to be considered; personal emotional baggage capable of contaminating relationships.

Psychologist Gary Sweeten calls this stuff our "squishy spots"—unresolved issues that open us to identifying too closely with another person. When this happens, we lose objectivity and the ability to discern clearly. When a group member's actions or words hit my squishy spots, "my feelings get mixed up with theirs, and I assume they feel about their situation the same way I feel about mine."[1] Or I assume that they're motivated by whatever is motivating me.

"Search me, O God, and know my heart; test me and know my anxious thoughts."
—Psalm 139:23

As leaders, it's important to remain alert to these issues. There are several ways to do this:

➤ **Pray.** Throughout this book, I advise you to pray before, during, and after acting. One reason for this admonition is to open your spirit to the wisdom of the Holy Spirit. As you are praying about how to handle a challenging person, ask God to search you and show you if there's anything in you that's causing you to perceive the situation incorrectly. If he points out an area of sin, wounding, or vulnerability, deal with that before you deal with the other person.

▶ **Seek accountability.** It's vital for you as a leader to be accountable to someone who has permission to ask any question and make any observation. This may be your prayer partner, co-leader, pastor, or spouse. But whomever God puts in that place, you need to listen to him or her. Before you confront a challenging person, check out your perceptions and ask if any of your stuff is getting in the way of your objectivity.

> "Why do you look at the speck of sawdust in your brother's eye and pay no attention to the plank in your own eye? How can you say to your brother, 'Let me take the speck out of your eye,' when all the time there is a plank in your own eye? You hypocrite, first take the plank out of your own eye, and then you will see clearly to remove the speck from your brother's eye." —Matthew 7:3-5

▶ **Receive healing.** In Chapter 1, I said that the leader always gains more than the group members. One of the ways this happens is that you continually have the opportunity to identify your squishy spots and take them to the Lord for healing. Depending on the issue, you may be able to do this alone, or you may need the ministry of another person. You may need to repent of a sinful behavior or attitude; you may need to ask forgiveness of another person. You may need to process childhood

Whatever the issue, know that God will be faithful to heal you if you ask in faith. Philippians 1:6 promises, "Being confident of this, that he who began a good work in you will carry it on to completion until the day of Christ Jesus." And 1 Thessalonians 5:24 reminds us, "The one who calls you is faithful and he will do it." If God has called you to leadership, he will be as faithful to provide healing for you as he is to provide it for your group members.

memories and identify lies that have held you in bondage for years.

Set a Goal of Restoration, Not Judgment

Your goal as you lead each person to maturity in Jesus Christ is to *restore*, not judge. The Greek word for restore in Galatians 6:1 refers to mending something that is broken. It was used to refer to mending torn fishing nets—a slow, tedious, and messy job.

> **Brothers, if someone is caught in a sin, you who are spiritual should restore him gently.**
> **—Galatians 6:1**

It's easy to judge one another. It's effortless for me to compare my sin with your sin so that I look more spiritual. But God's way is less about judging and more about restoration. When confronted with the woman caught in adultery, Jesus didn't pick up the first stone, nor did he affirm her behavior. He simply pointed out that there might be a few other sinners in the crowd, and then challenged her to go and sin no more.

Restoration may seem messy and slow. Frequently it is amazingly painful. But the authority you earn in the process of walking step by step and hand in hand through it is worth far more than being right.

Watch Your Language

Throughout this book, you'll be encouraged to talk to these challenging people. As a leader, you need to be bold enough to speak the truth in love to the people who are causing problems in the group. However, you must be ever so careful in *how* you do this.

It's so easy for these discussions to turn into heated debates or even shouting matches. It doesn't take much for an already wounded person to give up and leave the group in anger. As the

Caution

You may have the positional authority to discipline a group member, but such discipline seldom brings restoration. In fact, more often than not, it makes the mess bigger, the wound deeper, and the separation permanent. It shatters the sense of belonging and makes attachment much more difficult the next time. It forces the soul to rise up and protect itself.

leader, you'll walk a tightrope between healing and harming. As you approach a challenging person, remember the words of Galatians 6:1: "Brothers, if someone is caught in a sin, you who are spiritual should restore him gently. But watch yourself, or you also may be tempted" (emphasis added). Your goal is to lovingly restore the person, not to win the argument. Guard your heart and words to achieve this goal without being sucked into a confrontation. There are several skills that will serve you well as you offer tough love to your group members.

What's It Mean?

"I" messages: An "I" statement or message places the responsibility for and ownership of feelings with the speaker. It expresses how the speaker feels or what the speaker believes, rather than blaming another person for those feelings or beliefs.

➤ **Use "I" messages.** Whenever possible, frame your comments in "I" messages rather than "you" messages. What's the difference? In an "I" message, I take responsibility for my feelings and observations. In the process, I remain open to the possibility that I may be wrong. I'm willing to hear the other side of the issue. "You" messages, on the other hand, assume that the other person is wrong. They tend to cast blame. This immediately raises defenses and makes rational conversation very difficult.

For example, I would say, "I've observed…" or "I'm concerned …" rather than "You are…" or "You need to…" An "I" message keeps the conversation open and allows the other person to respond with less defensiveness than if he perceives that I'm accusing him of something. "I" messages leave the other person with their dignity intact.

➤ **Use Tentative Language.** In conjunction with "I" messages, consider using tentative language to create an atmosphere for dialogue rather than issuing an order. Since it's impossible to know exactly what another person is thinking, feeling, or experiencing, avoid being dogmatic in your language and tone. Tentative language offers respect to the other person by communicating an openness to listen to a response other than the one you expect. Some phrases that communicate tentative language include:

"It seems to me…"	**"Are you saying…"**
"I wonder if…?"	**"Are you feeling…"**
"Could it be that…?"	**"It sounds like…"**
"Is it possible that…?"	**"It appears that…"**

> **Watch your body language.** We communicate more with what we don't say than with what we do say. When there's conflict between words and body language, we almost always believe the body language. Nonverbal communication includes body movement, voice quality, and environmental surroundings.[3] It's important to understand the role of these elements in communication, especially when you need to talk with a challenging person.

Body movement. The head, face, mouth, shoulders, arms, legs, feet, and the whole body give clues to how both a speaker and a listener are feeling. When you need to offer correction, pay attention to your body as well as to the body of the person you're talking to. Try to keep your arms and legs uncrossed. Smile, if appropriate, but make sure it's genuine. Bottom line, remind yourself that you love this person. Even if you're uncomfortable, an open body will communicate warmth.

Robert Phipps defines *body language* as "the *unspoken communication* that goes on in every face-to-face encounter with another human being. It tells you their true feelings towards you and how well your words are being received. Between 60-80% of our message is communicated through our body language; only 7-10% is attributable to the actual words of a conversation."[2]

REMEMBER ...

"The eye is the lamp of the body. If your eyes are good, your whole body will be full of light."—Matthew 6:22

Eye contact. Your eyes are the windows to your soul and will communicate how you really feel, regardless of your words. Neuroscience has shown that when you meet a person, your left eye communicates with their left eye, which sends a neurological signal to the right side of the brain at the rate of six cycles per second.

This cycling is faster than any verbal or conscious communication, and both of you immediately know if you are being welcomed or rejected. So before you meet anyone from your group, remind yourself that this is a person beloved by God and by you. Communicate warmth and acceptance rather than rejection, and your words will carry more weight.

WHAT ARE YOU TRYING TO SAY?
Understanding Body Language

	GESTURE	WHAT IT CONVEYS	IF YOU'RE DOING IT
EYES	Avoiding Eye Contact	May mean she's shy. Or lying or trying to provoke you. May also be a nonverbal sign to cue someone to stop talking. May also be a cultural issue. In some cultures, avoiding eye contact is a sign of respect.	Unless you know of a cultural issue, always strive to maintain comfortable and gracious eye contact. Too much can make the listener feel under scrutiny and too little may indicate lack of interest on your part.
	Darting Eyes	Usually perceived as a sign of lying or hiding the truth.	Don't. Make comfortable eye contact.
	Rolling Eyes	Usually a sign of disrespect, condescension, disagreement, or frustration. Almost always an aggressive action.	Don't!
	Staring at You	Could be intense concentration, or could be rude and aggressive.	Be sure to break the gaze at comfortable intervals or when the listener breaks. You don't have to win the stare-down.
	Staring into Space	Could be intense concentration, or could indicate disagreement or disinterest. May be a "dissing" action or a nonverbal stop sign.	Don't. Train yourself to maintain comfortable eye contact.
FACE	Furrowing the Brow	May be a sign of thinking, disagreement, or questioning; or perhaps the listener can't hear or understand you.	Relax your face while talking. Clarify using words rather than gestures.
	Frowning	May mean the listener is unhappy or uncomfortable with the discussion. Or it might just indicate concentration or trying to figure something out.	Relax while talking. Smile and/or nod while listening. Clarify using words rather than gestures. Explain why you are frowning.
	Grimacing	Usually a sign of displeasure or discomfort. But it may just be a normal expression.	Relax your face and smile if appropriate. If something caught you off guard, explain your reaction.
	Lip Biting	May feel confused, perplexed, or uncomfortable. Or may be trying to come up with an answer—real or phony.	Relax and smile. Admit your discomfort.
	Lip Pursing	Pursing or twisting lips to the side may indicate thinking or an attempt to hold back an angry comment.	Relax and smile. Admit your discomfort.

GESTURE	WHAT IT CONVEYS	IF YOU'RE DOING IT
Tilted Head	When gently tilted to either side, this indicates friendliness or receptivity. When lifted high, it may indicate aloofness, disagreement, or resistance to your authority.	Watch your head position. Tilt slightly right or left, and slightly forward indicating your interest in what the person has to say.
Shoulder Shrug	May signal resignation, uncertainty, or surrender.	Try to be more definitive in your communication.
Squared Shoulders	Usually a sign of confidence and certainty, but may also be a sign of resistance	Relax and smile. Don't use your body to force your point.
Hunched Shoulders	May signal uncertainty or a cringing spirit.	Try to remain relaxed and confident. Remember that you are a child of God.
Crossed Arms	May be a conscious or subconscious effort to put distance or an emotional barrier between the speaker and listener. May indicate rejection of the speaker or idea. Or may just be the most comfortable position.	Consciously relax your arms and lean forward slightly. Try for an open position with arms at your side or behind your back.
Crossed Legs	May be a conscious or subconscious effort to put distance or an emotional barrier between the speaker and listener. May indicate rejection of the speaker or idea. Or may just be the most comfortable position.	Consciously relax your legs and lean forward slightly.
Tapping Feet or Legs	Probably indicates nervousness at a conscious or subconscious level.	Try to keep your feet and legs still. Your tapping will make other participants nervous.
Angle	People tend to angle toward those they like or agree with and away from those they dislike or disagree with	Be sure you aren't distancing yourself from the one to which you're speaking.
Comfort Zone	Each culture has a comfort zone—the distance we place between ourselves. Pay attention to how the person responds and how close they are comfortable being.e	Stay alert. If the other person backs up, you are too close; if they keep moving forward, they may want more closeness.
Slouching	May indicate disrespect or lack of interest. Or it may simply be an adapted position.	Stand or sit using good posture. Slouching can collapse the chest and make breathing more difficult, resulting in a feeling of nervousness.

HEAD

ARMS & HANDS

LEGS

POSTURE

Voice quality. Your voice level and pitch can communicate fear, embarrassment, pride, anger, frustration, or countless other emotions. Your voice tone can express disrespect and disdain, even when your words are gracious. Reminding yourself that the person you're talking to is another human being created in the image of God will help give your voice a healing tone rather than a harmful one.

Environmental surroundings. Throughout this book, I recommend that you find an appropriate time and place to talk to a challenging person. You want to avoid confronting or correcting a person in front of others or in a place that might cause embarrassment. Whenever possible, seek a neutral location and one that offers a sense of relaxation. You might go to a park or take a walk. You might find an office at church or invite the person to your home at a time when no one else is there. Avoid a restaurant or other public place if you feel that the conversation could turn heated or the person may cry. The key is to make the environment as *nonthreatening* as possible and to show respect to the feelings of the person you are correcting.

➤ Confront in person.

Because this is already an uncomfortable situation and because so much is communicated through body language, always try to talk to your challenging group member in person. Every step you take away from personal interaction gives you and them less data with which to work. So a telephone call loses the visual cues, and e-mail loses almost all non-verbals—as well as tone of voice. And since so many people are careless when writing e-mails, it's easy to miscommunicate this way. I've almost never had a good experience trying to resolve an issue via e-mail, and in fact, find that it usually just muddies the water.

> *A gentle answer turns away wrath, but a harsh word stirs up anger.*
> —Proverbs 15:1

➤ Avoid "always" and "never." It may seem as if the

person *always* monopolizes the discussion or *never* shows up on time, but as sure as you say that, she'll point out the one exception to the rule, and you'll end

Remember: Amost everyone responds better to encouragement than to accusation!

up arguing semantics rather than discussing the real issue. So avoid making global statements and even give the benefit of the doubt when you can. Again, using tentative language will help here.

> **Affirm rather than criticize.** It's easy to be critical of a person you perceive as creating problems in the group. Often by the time you're aware of the problem and muster the courage to say something, you're so irritated that your first impulse is to tell the person off. You think of all the things she's doing wrong and want to just make her stop. But remember, almost everyone responds better to encouragement than to accusation. So, find something to affirm before you criticize, and even when you correct, see if you can do it in an affirming way.

> **Avoid shaming.** Remember that any issue you face is about the behavior, not about the person. There's a critical difference between guilt and shame. Guilt deals with what a person *does*—the behavior. They may not even know they've erred until you talk to them, and they may be willing to correct the behavior as soon as it's brought to light. The usual and appropriate remedy for guilt is repentance and forgiveness. Shame, on the other hand, deals with who the person *is*—their very essence. There's no way to remedy shame because it cuts to the core of the person. Always confront the behavior, not the person.

WISE WORDS

"Shame is the soul-deep belief that something is horribly wrong with me that is not wrong with anyone else in the entire world. If I am bound by shame, I feel hopelessly, disgustingly different and worthless. I mean literally worth less than other people. ... Shame is rooted in the lie that human beings can and should be perfect."[4]

—**Sandra D. Wilson,** *Hurt People Hurt People*

> ➤ **Use active listening.** Often in conversations that are uncomfortable, we're so busy thinking about the next thing we want to say that we don't hear what the other person is saying. Sometimes we even talk over any attempt to explain. Develop the habit of active listening, where you attend to the conversation with your whole body and mind, and then reflect back to the person what you heard. Stop periodically and say, "What I hear you saying is… Is that correct?" Make sure that you clearly understand the other person's perspective before continuing.

Remember, the goal in using these skills is to lovingly restore, not to prove you are right.

CHECK OUT THESE KEY POINTS!

Deal with your own stuff first.

Set a goal of restoration, not judgment.

Use "I" messages & tentative language.

Check your body language & that of others.

Treat others as valued & beloved in God's image.

[1] Dr. Gary R. Sweeten with Craig Fendley, *Apples of Gold: Developing the Fruit of the Spirit for Life and Ministry* (Cincinnati: Equipping Ministries International, 1983), p. 35.

[2] Robert Phipps, Body Language Training: Shedding Light on Body Language. http://www.bodylanguagetraining.com/

[3] These concepts are discussed in Sweeten, *Apples of Gold*, pp. 44, 45.

[4] Sandra D. Wilson, *Hurt People Hurt People* (Grand Rapids: Discovery House Publishers, 2001), pp. 16, 17.

Discussion 3 Challenges

Most of the discussion challenges you'll face are simple: how to get people to talk—or stop talking. These tips will give you the confidence you need to keep the discussion moving.

MONA MONOPOLY—THE CHRONIC TALKER

Mona Monopoly is a natural extrovert. She's also quite well versed in Scripture and has a lot of good points to make. The problem is that she makes them all the time. Every time you ask a question, Mona jumps in with the answer before anyone else even has time to think about it. And her answers go on and on and on. People start checking their watches; the leaves change from green to orange; your co-leader's hair turns grey. You're finding that you can't get through the discussion you've planned because she's so long-winded. Others in the group have pretty much given up trying to answer a question. They simply watch you and Mona dialogue. What can you do?

❶ **Pray for Mona.** As you pray for the various members of your group during your personal prayer time, pray that the Lord would show Mona how her behavior is affecting the group. Pray for her to be sensitive to the Holy Spirit and allow him to correct her talkativeness. The writer of Proverbs 10:19 proposed a correlation between sin and the number of words we speak. It certainly is true that the more words Mona says, the more likely she is to offend someone in the group. And that becomes your problem.

"When words are many, sin is not absent, but he who holds his tongue is wise." —Proverbs 10:19

❷ **Ask for short answers.** Ask the group, "In one or two sentences, what does the author mean?" Be specific about the information you want and the fact that you want short answers. Do this often to reinforce your desire for brief responses.

❸ **Ask for several responses.** Use this in combination with asking for short answers. For example, you might say, "I'd like several of you to comment briefly on…"

❹ **Call on someone else first.** While I don't usually like to put people on the spot by calling on them, it may be necessary to break Mona's habit and give someone else a chance to speak. I'll do this several times, calling on various people, and then call on Mona last.

❺ **Use a printed schedule.** This puts everyone on notice what you want to accomplish during the meeting and the approximate times you expect to reach each transition. If Mona starts her monologue, you can simply say, "I'd love to hear more, Mona, but we need to stay on schedule if we hope to leave by 9:00." Of course, she probably doesn't want to leave by 9:00, but others do.

WiSe Words

"He that cannot refrain from much speaking is like a city without walls."
—Sir Walter Raleigh

❻ **Interrupt if necessary.** You've probably been told it's not polite to interrupt, but sometimes you must if you want to give others a chance to answer. After Mona has made a couple of good points or when she begins to repeat herself, simply jump in and rather forcefully (but kindly) say, "Thanks, Mona. That's a great point. Jane, what do you think about that?"

❼ **Talk to her.** Those who chatter on and on usually miss the nonverbal cues that most listeners send. When listeners are getting bored, they will

> If Mona begins to ramble, she's probably thinking as she's speaking rather than thinking *before* she speaks. This may be a sign of an undisciplined mind or someone who has never learned to plan her comments. This is also common with those who are not listened to (or have no one to talk to) at home. Again you need to be assertive. Interject by saying, "Wait a minute, Mona. You're throwing out a lot of good ideas, but I'm afraid we'll lose track of them. Could you take one point, boil it down to one sentence, and then let's see what the others think about it?"

reduce eye contact to a minimum or stare off into space. Be alert for these signs of frustration from members of your group. Even if Mona misses them, you'll know it's time to give her a gentle remedial class on nonverbal stop signs.

Refer to the table on pages 24, 25 (*What Are You Trying to Say? Understanding Body Language*) for some nonverbal stop signs.

Find a time when you can meet with Mona privately in a casual, neutral setting. Affirm her and appeal to her desire to help you and the others. Be honest, but in a positive way. Say something like, "Mona, I really appreciate the way you always come prepared and with such good responses. I can tell you're getting a lot out of this study. Now I need your help. Have you noticed that it takes some of the other members a bit longer to come up with their answers than it does you? When you jump right in with such thorough answers, the others feel they don't have anything to add. In fact, I think they might be a bit intimidated. I was wondering what would happen if you'd hold back a bit? Do you think maybe Jane or Karen would feel more comfortable answering?"

❽ **Ask her to help as a co-leader or leader-in-training.** If Mona has most of the qualities of leadership, perhaps she is being underutilized. Always be on the lookout for potential leaders or leaders-in-training. If you already have a co-leader or leader-in-training, what about adding more than one? Give her some additional responsibility in the group to begin affirming her. Work with her. Train her. Remind her that, as a leader-in-training, it's more important to encourage others to answer than to have the answer herself.

Caution

Be wise in your decision. Some Monas don't have the maturity to be a co-leader. They're using their skills at monopoly to cover their own insecurity or spiritual immaturity.

When I was a new small group leader, I found suggestions like the ones I've given in this chapter difficult. What I learned was that my discomfort was a result of my reluctance to take charge and lead my group. Once I realized that group members craved a leader, I gained the confidence to take steps to make the group work for everyone. So go ahead. Be the leader and give everyone a chance to talk.

SOUNDS OF SILENCE — THE QUIET GROUP

Perhaps you're facing the opposite of Mona. Perhaps your group responds to each question with deafening silence. You ask a question, and after what seems like an eon, no one has ventured a response. You look around for signs of life, but everyone is diligently studying the design in the carpet. This problem is especially common in a new group or in the first few minutes of a discussion. Now what?

> There is a time for everything, and a season for every activity under heaven: …a time to be silent and a time to speak.
> —Ecclesiastes 3:1, 7

1. Pray for your group and for your understanding. Pray first that the Lord would show you the barriers to discussion. Be willing to have him show you any error you're making in leading the discussion. Then ask him for specific wisdom in working with your group. You'll be amazed at what he shows you as you're faithful to pray.

2. Don't rush to fill the void. Sometimes, in our desire to be a great leader, we see silence as our enemy. Realize that you're better prepared than anyone else and you know where the discussion is going. Your group members don't.

If the silent treatment begins after your group has been meeting and functioning well for some time, assume there's a serious problem or offense that needs to be addressed. Often by simply admitting that there seems to be a problem and offering to talk about it, you can figure out the problem and address it. Say something like, "Something doesn't feel right. What's going on?" or "This isn't like you guys. Is there something I'm missing?" If no one is willing to tell you, you'll need to do some detective work. A sudden change in the behavior of a whole group is a pretty clear signal that something's wrong.

Be sure to allow enough time for people to gather their thoughts and formulate an answer, especially for the first few questions. Realize that they need time to hear the question, understand it, process it, decide if their answer makes sense in relation to the rest of the discussion, and open their mouths. That can easily take 15 to 20 seconds—longer if you've asked a question that isn't in the study guide. But to you, 20 seconds feels like an eternity!

TRY THIS!

Don't be afraid of silence. Let it reign for at least 20 to 30 seconds before you come to the rescue. Stop now and time how long 20 seconds feels. No wonder you jump in!

What usually happens is that after 5 to 10 seconds, the uncomfortable leader will rephrase the question or give an answer. That fills the silence and relieves everyone's distress. Instead, try letting the silence continue. Sit comfortably. Glance at a few people, your face inviting and anticipating their responses, but don't open your mouth. Before you know it the tension will prompt someone else to end the discomfort, and he or she will answer. Chances are, the discussion will be off and running.

3. Draw out members. After you've allowed a reasonable silence, call on someone. Don't zero in on the shiest or quietest member. Aim for the mid-range. Look for people whose eyes tell you they have an answer. Then smile and gently ask, "Tom, what do you think?" If Tom says he doesn't know or passes, allow that. Try him again later, but allow him to maintain his dignity by not putting him on the spot.

For more ideas on phrasing good questions, see the Small Group HELP! Guide, Now That's a Good Question, by Terry Powell (Standard Publishing).

4. Be sure your question is clear. Sometimes people don't answer because they don't understand the question, but they don't want to appear stupid by asking for clarification.

Be sure to allow enough time for people to gather their thoughts and formulate an answer, especially for the first few questions.

I use a lesson plan to help me structure the discussion. When preparing, be sure to double-check your questions for clarity. Then during the study, if you think a question is unclear, ask, "Does this question make sense?" or "Maybe I didn't say that too well. Let me try again." Then rephrase the question. But the key is to use that as a last resort—not within the first 20 to 30 seconds. Once the group is comfortable with one another, someone will let you know if a question isn't clear.

5. Answer in pairs. In the unlikely case that your entire group is totally introverted and everyone has a hard time with discussion, try breaking them into smaller, more comfortable groups. Make groups of two and have them answer the question to each other. Next time, switch the people around. Then break into groups of three or four. Gradually move into larger groups as people become more comfortable with one another.

It's an unusual group that won't warm up and begin talking when you take these steps. Soon they'll be talking so much you'll wonder why you ever worried.

QUENTIN QUIET — THE SILENT PERSON

Your group as a whole is responding well, but Quentin Quiet never says a word. You know he comes prepared, but he never opens his mouth in front of the group. You don't want to ignore him, but you also don't want to push him. *What can you do?*

"Even a fool is thought wise if he keeps silent, and discerning if he holds his tongue."

—Proverbs 17:28

First, understand that some people are quiet because, one way or another, silence works for them. Here are some possibilities, as outlined by Robert M. Bramson in *Coping with Difficult People:*[1]

► For some, being quiet is a noncommittal way to handle potentially painful interpersonal situations. If I'm uncomfortable with the topic, the group, or a group member, being quiet is often the easiest way to cope.

► For others, silence may represent calculated or passive aggression. It's an easy way to hurt or control people, especially if the quiet person is skilled at this approach. This technique may be directed at you, someone else in the group, or life in general.

> For many, silence is a way of avoiding themselves. Spoken words give concrete reality to thoughts and feelings.

Once you understand more about the reasons Quentin never opens his mouth, you're in a better position to intervene if his reason is one of the problematic ones.

> "There is one who keeps silent because he has no answer, while another keeps silent because he knows when to speak."
> —Sirach 20:6 *(Revised Standard Version)*

1. Pray for Quentin. In your personal prayer time, pray that the Lord would give Quentin the same freedom to talk that the other group members have. Pray for wisdom to understand any specific barriers, including those that may be caused by you or other members of the group.

2. Spend time with him outside of the meeting. Make a point of talking with Quentin before or after the group time. Chat with him during refreshments. Meet for lunch if you can. Let him see you as a friend. If you have a co-leader or leader-in-training, encourage him or her to do the same. Then bring another person or two into that circle, perhaps during refreshments. Before long, Quentin may forget how shy he is and be comfortable enough to risk an answer.

> "To articulate to another, or to yourself, secret fears or aspirations is to face the fact that you have them. How much safer to keep the words safely unspoken, to mask it all by feeling confused, and to skirt the whole issue by remaining close-lipped, letting others fill the silence."[2]
> —Robert M. Bramson, *Coping with Difficult People*

3. Call on him. If Quentin was raised under the philosophy "Children should be seen and not heard" or "Speak only when spoken to," maybe he's just waiting for you to give him permission to talk. Some people feel that what they have to say isn't very important, but if you ask their opinion, they'll give it.

Why Didn't You Warn Me? **35**

Find a question you know he can answer or one that simply asks his opinion. Open-ended questions have a better chance of drawing out more than a yes, no, or nod. Smile and say, "Quentin, what do you think about…?" Give him time to formulate his answer. Affirm even the shortest and most hesitant response. But also give him the freedom to pass if he wishes.

4. Go around the circle. I usually avoid this approach, but it's one way to open up a quiet member. Find a question you'd like to concentrate on and say, "I think this is an important question. Let's have everyone respond in just one or two sentences." Start at a point where Quentin won't be first or last, but a little past midway. You've reinforced that you want short answers, so he knows he won't have to give an oration. Affirm each response to build his self-confidence. You won't want to use this approach often, but once in awhile it may work to break down his barriers. If he passes, simply smile and move on. You don't want to put him on the spot.

5. Give him a job. Ask Quentin to pour coffee, greet newcomers, read Scripture, or help plan a group activity. As he becomes involved in the life of the group, he may forget to remain quiet.

6. Use the friendly, silent stare. If you sense there's a bit of passive aggressive behavior or resistance at play, simply look at Quentin with a quizzical, expectant expression on your face, eyebrows raised, eyes wide as if waiting for a response. Since he may regard direct eye contact as a push or a demand, focus in a neutral area of the face—the lips or chin, for example. You may need to maintain this look beyond your comfort level, but eventually most Quentins will be prompted to respond. As with the silent group, the key is not to fill the silence.

> ### Consider This…
> Some perceptive people are quiet out of deference to the group. These people command a presence that gives the impression that once they've spoken, everything that needs to be said has been said. They may be imposing because of their physical size, breadth of knowledge, or position. Such people often remain quiet simply to allow others to have the opportunity to respond.

7. Recognize that Quentin may be a truly wise person. Don't naturally assume that the quiet person isn't very smart. Sometimes they have a lot to say but don't need to say it all the time. You'll know this is the case if, when he does speak, his comments are deep and pertinent.

It's easy to overlook the single silent person, but the astute leader will work at discerning why Quentin is so quiet and then enfolding him into the discussion.

POLLY PRAYERLESS—THE PERSON WHO WON'T PRAY ALOUD

Polly Prayerless contributes well to the group, but she simply won't pray aloud. In fact, before the first meeting she warned you that she wasn't one to pray in a group. There could be several reasons for this reluctance. Understanding them will help you encourage a person like Polly.

> *"One day Jesus was praying in a certain place. When he finished, one of his disciples said to him, 'Lord, teach us to pray.'"*
> —Luke 11:1

✤ Praying aloud is new for many people, especially new Christians. It's scary to hear your own voice talking to God. If your group includes new Christians or people whose religious backgrounds don't include audible prayer or conversational prayer as opposed to prayers read from a book, be gentle and patient with them.

✤ Others feel intimidated. Like Moses in Exodus 4:10, some think they're not eloquent enough to speak to God. They feel "slow of speech and tongue." This is particularly true when others in your group eloquently and effortlessly pray on and on in the King's English. It's also common when there are wide educational differences among members of your group.

✤ Some people are just naturally shy. It's not that they have anything against prayer. It's that they don't like talking aloud to anyone. They weigh every word and measure every sentence but always feel they've come up short.

The key to handling a reluctant pray-er is sensitivity. Put yourself in her shoes and don't pressure her. What are some ways of doing this?

1. Pray for Polly. Pray privately that Polly will gain confidence. While audible prayer isn't the most important thing you'll accomplish in the group, learning this skill may make Polly feel better about herself. Often the people who are most reluctant to pray out loud don't feel very good about who they are on other levels as well.

2. Let everyone know that they're under no compulsion to pray aloud. Before the prayer times in your first few meetings, specifically state that you understand that not everyone is comfortable praying audibly. Affirm that their silent prayers are as effective as audible prayers, but that you encourage members to join in when they feel comfortable. Assume that after several weeks even Polly will be comfortable enough to pray aloud.

3. Keep prayer conversational. While some people are comfortable praying in King James English, others will be terrified of making a mistake or not sounding spiritual enough. If some in your group always pray in a formal, stilted tone, break the mold by being contemporary, conversational, and even familiar as you pray.

4. Encourage short sentence prayers. If you think the long-winded prayers of others might be intimidating Polly, encourage everyone in the group to keep prayers brief and to the point. Do the same yourself. And allow Polly to pray silently for as long as she needs to.

5. Break into smaller groups for prayer. After Polly has become comfortable with the group in every other way, try breaking into groups of three for prayer. Let people choose their own partners, or pair Polly with the person she's closest to. Sometimes it's easier to break the silence with just a couple of close friends. If yours is a couples group, consider breaking into gender-based groups for prayer. You'll get a lot more freedom from the reluctant pray-ers. Again, affirm each person's right to pray silently.

6. Don't go around the circle. If you do, Polly will spend the entire time in terror, counting the number of people until it's her turn. And the person after her, knowing of her reluctance, won't know whether to wait or rescue her. If you see that prayer is beginning to go around the circle, jump in and pray out of turn to break it up—even if you've already prayed once.

7. Don't call on Polly to open or close in prayer. Ask for volunteers if you feel you need to assign certain roles.

8. Don't treat Polly differently from those who pray audibly. Let her know that she is loved and valued just as she is.

9. Model prayers that reflect your honest feelings. If you're angry, don't minimize your feelings by telling God you're "bothered"

Let group members know they're valued just as they are.

or a "little concerned." Tell him how furious you are. Be real and you'll encourage your entire group, but especially Polly.

I've never yet seen this combination fail to eventually produce a confident, outgoing person. And some of my most reluctant pray-ers have gone on to assume leadership in the next group!

WiSe Words

"He who has learned to pray has learned the greatest secret of a holy and a happy life."
—William Law

OK, now you're equipped to deal with the most common small group challenges, but, as you've probably already figured out, there are others that are a little stickier. Meet a few more challenging people in Chapter 4.

1. Robert M. Bramson, *Coping with Difficult People* (New York, NY: Doubleday, 1981), p. 71.

2. Bramson, p. 71

More Discussion Challenges

Sometimes the toughest challenges in leading a discussion are with people who, in one way or another, tend to disrupt the discussion. Most of these disruptions aren't deliberate, but you may feel they are. Here are some tips to keep your group on track.

RHONDA RABBITRAIL—THE PERSON WHO DOESN'T STAY ON TRACK

Rhonda Rabbitrail is fun to have in your group. She's bright, witty, and quite intelligent. But it seems that no matter what question you ask, she's suddenly taking the discussion off on a tangent. Sometimes you don't even realize this until the discussion is miles from where you intended to go. Her questions are always interesting, but they never go in the direction you had planned. She's like a hunting dog that catches the scent of a rabbit and is off chasing it instead of following the fox. How can you avoid going off on Rhonda's rabbit trails?

"But the fruit of the Spirit is... self-control."
—Galatians 5:22, 23

1. Pray for Rhonda.

Most Rhondas aren't being malicious or trying to confuse you. There's a good chance that Rhonda is scattered in every area of her life. Pray that she will see this as an area for growth. Pray for wisdom in helping her grow.

Download a sample lesson plan from www.whydidntyouwarnme.com. Feel free to adapt this to your needs.

2. Be clear about your goal for the discussion.

It's essential to have a goal or direction for each meeting. If you don't have a plan, you won't realize until it's too late that the discussion is off on a tangent. When I'm leading a group, I like to use a lesson plan to clarify my own thoughts and to make sure the discussion stays on track. If Rhonda is in your group, it's especially important to communicate your goal clearly. Start the discussion by saying, "There are several interesting points in today's lesson, but the one I think would be most beneficial for us to pursue is…" That puts everyone on notice that you'd rather not pursue the other "interesting points."

3. Take the subtle approach.

In the early weeks of the group, you may want to take an indirect approach. When you realize that Rhonda is chasing rabbits, let her finish and then redirect the question to another member of the group. Affirm Rhonda without encouraging her: "Thanks for that interesting point, Rhonda. Now, Chris, what do you think about…?" This may be a good place to call on your co-leader, who shouldn't be intimidated by being called on.

WiSe Words

If you don't know where you're going, any road will take you there. —Familiar Proverb

4. Nip it as soon as you recognize it.

You may need to progress to this strategy if Rhonda doesn't take the hint in your first couple of tries to get her back on track. As soon as you realize she's chasing rabbits again, interrupt and move the discussion back on track. You can affirm her by saying, "That's an interesting point, Rhonda. I wish we had more time to explore it.

It's essential to have a goal or direction for each meeting. Don't wait until it's too late and the discussion is off on a tangent.

But I'm not sure I see how that relates to the question of…"

By taking responsibility for your failure to see the connection, you don't embarrass Rhonda. You allow her to make the connection—if there is one. If there isn't, suggest that perhaps you can discuss her point after the meeting. When Rhonda is in your group, hold on to the reins, or you'll find yourself and your group being dragged hither and yon. It'll be an interesting ride, but not necessarily useful. So follow these tips to stay on the right track!

LINDA LAZY & BUDDY BUSY— THE PEOPLE WHO WON'T STUDY

Linda Lazy and Buddy Busy have similar problems. They seldom do their homework. Linda just isn't interested, and Buddy can't seem to fit it into his 60-item to-do list. The problem is that group discussions work best when everyone prepares. How do you handle this?

• **Pray for your group, especially Linda and Buddy.** It's hard to find time to do a Bible study lesson, particularly if it's new on your schedule. Pray that it will become such a priority for these members that they will find the time somewhere. Also recognize that this may be the work of the enemy in Linda's or Buddy's life. Satan will do almost anything to keep God's people out of God's Word. Laziness and busyness are equal enemies. Some aggressive spiritual warfare may be called for.

> Some groups do not require homework between meetings. But if you do give homework, realize that this may cause challenges because of those who won't or can't keep up.

• **Remind group members of the need to do their homework.** If participating in a facilitated discussion group is new to your members, you may need to remind them that you aren't going to teach the lesson. If no one does the homework, the discussion will flounder. Make this reminder gently and frequently at the beginning or end of the group time, or send a midweek e-mail encouraging participants to stay current in their homework and in applying what they've been learning. Hopefully you'll break a bad habit before it starts.

- **Ignore it.** If I only have one or two such people in an otherwise conscientious group, I often simply ignore it unless Linda or Buddy begin to cause problems by their lack of preparation. I've found that they usually won't volunteer an answer they don't know, and sometimes the frustration of being unprepared will motivate them. And I understand that simply showing up is an effort for many people, so I try to offer some grace whenever possible. If the disease begins to spread to others who think, *if Linda can get away with not doing her homework, I can too*, take more definitive action.

> Tell group members you want them to come and participate even if they haven't done their homework. Most people can benefit from the discussion even if they haven't studied the lesson, and I believe that the continuity of the group is more important than doing one's homework.

- **Refuse to allow participation.** This is an optional technique used by some successful Bible study ministries. If you don't do your homework, you're welcome to sit in on the discussion, but you can't talk. It can be effective and offers an incentive for most people to try a little harder to schedule time to do homework, but it can easily become legalistic. It can also serve as an excuse to stay home for those who aren't fully committed. Make a decision about this approach when your group begins and include it in the group covenant if you think it's important.

> " Beware of squatting lazily before God instead of putting up a glorious fight so that you may lay hold of His strength. "
> —Oswald Chambers, *My Utmost for His Highest*

- **Reevaluate the workload.** If several people are having difficulty getting their homework done, you may want to reevaluate the workload. Though most studies take an hour or less per week to do, even that may overwhelm new Christians or those whose lives are especially hectic.

To lighten the time commitment in studies I've led, I've taken two weeks for each lesson. In one group, we went through the entire lesson in the first week and then specifically applied that lesson to our lives the second week. Meanwhile, the participants could begin the next chapter, giving them two weeks to complete it. In another group, we divided the lesson and took two or three weeks to complete a chapter.

- **Do a little every day.** Encourage everyone to spend some time each day working on the lesson rather than leaving it until the night before your group meeting. This has two advantages. First, it gets them into the Word every day—a worthy goal in itself. And second, it prevents the problem of their having nothing done when something else comes up the night before. And it will.

Some people will honestly be surprised and encouraged at suggestions like "turn off the TV," "do it on your lunch hour," or "insist that your children take a quiet time or nap every afternoon."

- **Brainstorm the options.** If several people are finding it difficult to complete their homework, take a few minutes at the beginning of a meeting and brainstorm how people can meet their obligations. Sometimes simply hearing how others do it can offer new ideas for those who are mentally or emotionally locked into one way of doing Bible study. Encourage your group members to become creative problem solvers. This approach is particularly helpful for members who are in a new situation—new moms, employed people trying their first study, or people recovering from a lengthy illness, for example.

Having a couple of people who don't do their homework isn't a critical problem. But if your goal is to get your group in the habit of studying the Bible, regular homework is a good way to accomplish it.

WILLY WRONG—THE PERSON WHO DOESN'T UNDERSTAND

Willy Wrong seldom has the right answer—even if there are several possible ones. Sometimes it seems as if he's answering a different question than the one you asked. He's not trying to be funny, but sometimes it ends up that way. You want to cringe every time he opens his mouth. After all, how could anyone come up with the answers he does?

> "Who can discern his errors? Forgive my hidden faults."
> —Psalms 19:12

Maybe he's just slow or socially handicapped. I've known many Willys who have spent much of their lives in such social isolation that they simply don't know how to communicate in a group situation. Or perhaps he's new to the Bible and Christian terms and honestly doesn't know that his responses would fit better at a New Age gathering. Maybe Willy doesn't listen well or even has an auditory processing disorder. You hate to embarrass the guy, but *what can you do?*

1. Pray for discernment. There could be many reasons for Willy's problems. Pray for wisdom to identify just why he's always so far off base. That will help you to deal sensitively with him.

2. Offer to study with him. If Willy seems genuinely concerned and wants to benefit from the group, you or your co-leader can offer to study with him a time or two. That may help you understand where he's going wrong. Does he read or hear well enough to understand the questions? Does he appear to have some sort of learning disability or neurological problem? If so, is he aware of his problem and is he getting help? Are there ways you can help him? Or does he simply lack Christian understanding and will outgrow his odd comments in time?

3. Affirm him even while correcting. Whether or not you can get to the source of the problem, don't embarrass him. Rather, model a loving attitude and teach your group how to serve those who are different. This is essential to any healing he might receive from the group. If he gives a wrong answer (and Willy usually isn't shy, so he will), smile and say, "That's an interesting perspective, Willy. And Ted, what do you think?"

4. Ask Willy to respond to questions you're certain he can answer. As much as I dislike asking specific people to answer questions, you may want to throw Willy the questions you know— or hope—he can handle. Perhaps these will be application or opinion questions as opposed to objective or interpretive ones. Pay attention to him and try to learn the type of questions he's better at. Give him as much potential for success as you can, and hope that he won't also try to answer those questions he has more problems with. The idea is to build his confidence by giving him opportunities to succeed.

5. Just love him. I've seen some Willys grow and change as we've applied these techniques. Others simply don't have the mental or emotional ability to do so. If Willy's responses aren't causing a major problem in the group, this is a time to practice love and grace. Willy's soul will grow from the love of the group, and the benefits he'll gain from being part of the community will bring some level of healing to him. And your group will also grow as members learn to forebear in a difficult situation. Never allow your desire for perfection in your group to override mercy to someone who is trying in good faith to participate. Dealing with Willy is a situation where you are called to bear one another's burdens and offer grace.

If Willy's answers are not only wrong but could also cause misunderstanding, misinterpretation, or a theological problem, don't let them stand. But if another group member can clear up the confusion by inserting another opinion or answer, that's better than your saying, "Oh no, Willy. You're wrong again!"

YOLANDA YAWNER—THE BORED PERSON

Yolanda Yawner is always bored. You can see it in her eyes. You can hear it in her yawns. You know it for sure when she pulls out her cell phone and starts text messaging her boyfriend. You're not sure why she's here, but she sure doesn't contribute much. How do you keep her attitude from infecting the rest of the group?

1. Pray for insight. As with so many of the other problems, take Yolanda to the one who knows why she's behaving this way. Pray to receive a heart of wisdom and insight. Pray for gentleness and graciousness as you work with her.

2. Do a "boring" check. Maybe your group is boring. Before you get too upset with Yolanda, be sure that the group warrants her attention. Perhaps, as in one group I led years ago, the study guide is intellectually insulting or spiritually dry. Perhaps the members have no interest in it. Perhaps your questions or attitude suggest a lack of interest or excitement.

Casually ask others how they're enjoying the group. Ask what you might do to make it more interesting. If you hear a valid complaint, you'll all benefit from making the necessary changes. I did this in the boring study I led and learned that people loved the group but hated the particular study guide we were using. We scrapped the published study guide, and I wrote questions that drew the members to apply the Scripture to life. It made a huge difference, and Yolanda put her cell phone away.

3. Try to figure out why she's reacting like this. The bored attitude might be normal for a high school student who couldn't care less about the group, but Mom insists she attend. Even if Yolanda is an adult, her attitude may be a carryover from adolescent behavior. Or, it may be that Yolanda is backsliding or grappling with a major spiritual issue. She may be hurting deeply, but puts on the bored veneer to keep you and everyone else out. On the other hand, Yolanda may simply not realize the message her behavior is communicating.

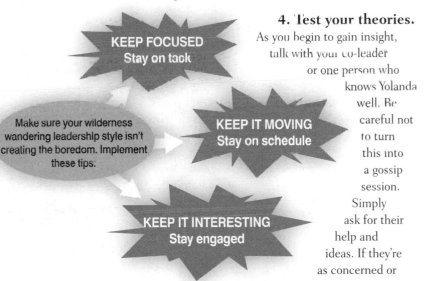

4. Test your theories. As you begin to gain insight, talk with your co-leader or one person who knows Yolanda well. Be careful not to turn this into a gossip session. Simply ask for their help and ideas. If they're as concerned or

KEEP FOCUSED
Stay on task

Make sure your wilderness wandering leadership style isn't creating the boredom. Implement these tips:

KEEP IT MOVING
Stay on schedule

KEEP IT INTERESTING
Stay engaged

bothered as you are, you'll need to take it to the group. However, you may find that Yolanda is just triggering one of your pet peeves, and her behavior isn't as annoying as you thought.

5. Take it to the group. Start your next meeting by saying, "Before we begin, we need to do some family business. I've become concerned about what appears to be a lack of attention or an attitude of boredom within the group. I want us to work together, but I don't feel we can if everyone isn't functioning at about the same level of enthusiasm. How are you feeling about the way our group is functioning?" This conversation will be easier if you can address several problems, such as people coming late or leaving early, irregular attendance, and people not preparing for the study.

If Yolanda feels singled out, she'll either be very quiet, hoping to fade into the upholstery, or she'll react with anger. Be prepared for both. Ultimately, the group will need to set guidelines that everyone agrees to abide by. If you have made a group covenant, you may want to briefly review it at this time.

> "When people are bored, it is primarily with their own selves that they are bored."
>
> —Eric Hoffer, *The True Believer: Thoughts on the Nature of Mass Movements* (1951)

6. Talk to Yolanda. If the group improves but Yolanda doesn't, pray for grace and then find time to talk with her privately. You may want to schedule lunch, coffee, or a walk after church. You want enough privacy and time to be able to serve her. Begin the conversation lovingly and gently. Avoid any hint of anger or malice. After appropriate small talk, you might say, "Yolanda, I've noticed that you seem to be a bit bored by the group. I'm wondering if I can do anything to help you enjoy it more."

Maybe she'll respond; maybe she won't. Maybe she won't have any idea what you're talking about,

Listen with your heart as well as your head.

especially if "bored" is her natural affect. Maybe she'll hit you with both barrels. If so, her charges may or may not be valid. Maintain your composure. Listen with your heart as well as your head. Don't accept unnecessary blame, but also don't fight back. Let her know you love her and want to help her in any way you can. Ask for her help in creating a more positive atmosphere in the group.

7. Set some guidelines. If Yolanda's behavior or attitude is truly disruptive and she hasn't responded to the group covenant or discussion, you'll need to be very direct with her, identifying the problem behavior, why it's disruptive, and how you expect her to change. The key is increasing her sensitivity to the group, so focus on how her behavior is disruptive and specific actions needed to remedy the problems.

Yolanda's attitude can be frustrating when you want everyone to love your group. Don't go overboard trying to entertain everyone, but remain alert to ways of making your meetings more interesting.

CLANCY CLICHÉ —THE PERSON WHO USES JARGON

WHAT DOES IT MEAN?

Clancy Cliché has a well-worn answer for everything. He's full of jargon, especially Christianese, and his responses seldom convey much of anything. He's quick to offer a pious non-answer, but you can't get him to delve deeply enough beneath the surface to solicit a meaningful response. He always has advice for people with prayer requests, and it's usually something like, "Just trust and obey, and everything will turn out OK." You wish you could hide behind the nearest sofa! How can you reach Clancy?

Christianese: Vocabulary that is unique to or has a unique meaning to Christians, or sometimes to narrow groups of Christians. These words may be meaningless or confusing to those from other backgrounds or persuasions.

> "But I tell you that men will have to give account on the day of judgment for every careless word they have spoken." —Matthew 12:36

1. Pray for Clancy. Pray first for wisdom and insight into why Clancy uses so much jargon. Maybe he's never learned to articulate, but maybe he's got a deeper problem he's hiding. Only the Holy Spirit can give you the wisdom, insight, and gentleness you'll need.

Why Didn't You Warn Me? **49**

2. Ask for clarification. Especially if Clancy grew up in the church, phrases like "saved by the blood," "justification," "the throne of grace," and "propitiation" may be part of his normal vocabulary. Maybe he knows what they mean; maybe he doesn't. The best way to find out is to ask him to clarify. Say, "Could you expand a bit more on that, Clancy? How does taking our requests to the throne of grace apply to this question?" or, "When you say we're justified by faith, what does that mean to you?" You may need to ask several follow-up questions before you get an answer that most members of the group understand. This may seem tedious, but you're also modeling the type of answer you want. Hopefully as the group continues, Clancy and all the members will respond with more definitive answers.

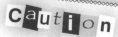

Make sure you aren't using jargon. Be alert to this possibility as you prepare to lead, especially if your study guide uses Christianese.

3. Explain why it's important to give concrete responses.

The whole group may need to understand why you continue to probe when someone responds with jargon or a cliché. Say, "You may wonder why I ask for clarification to these responses. It's because I really want to make sure we all understand one another. Sometimes when we give an answer that's too familiar, different people understand it in different ways. I want to be sure we all understand each answer in the context of our discussion."

While dealing with Clancy may seem tedious, you'll find that your discussions go deeper and are more meaningful when everyone is speaking the same language.

4. Encourage prayer rather than answers.

When Clancy gives his "trust and obey" response to a prayer request, remind the group that we aren't here to solve problems or even to say something in response to the prayer needs. We are simply here to pray. Of course, you'll want to do this for everyone, not just for Clancy.

You've learned how to deal with a variety of sticky discussion issues, but some challenges are even more deeply rooted. In Chapter 5 I'll show you how to deal with some real characters!

Character 5 Challenges

Every now and then, a participant's basic character causes challenges. This person is more difficult to deal with, but it's essential for the health of your group that you recognize the challenge and take action quickly. These tips will give you the confidence to face them and protect your group.

In This Chapter...

- Griselda Gossip—
  The Person Who Breaks Confidentiality
- Charlie Challenge—
  The Argumentative Person
- Audrey Arrogant—
  The Dogmatic Person
- Sidney Sinner—
  The Unrepentant Person

GRISELDA GOSSIP— THE PERSON WHO BREAKS CONFIDENTIALITY

Griselda Gossip can't help herself. Every time someone in the group discloses a deep personal need, Griselda finds someone else to tell. She isn't malicious. In fact, she's usually just sharing a prayer request that isn't hers to share.

> **A gossip betrays a confidence, but a trustworthy man keeps a secret.**
> **—Proverbs 11:1**

The problem for your group is that this is a violation of the confidentiality principle that should be a part of your group covenant (see Appendix).

Confidentiality is a key concept of group effectiveness. It's essential if you want people to have the freedom to openly share their weaknesses and seek accountability for growth and maturity. And the more wounded or needy the people in your group are, the more critical this issue becomes. When word of a leak gets back to the members, they stop being open and the group begins to lose its vitality.

Sometimes your first clue that there is a problem is when Griselda is sharing the prayer requests of someone who is not even in your group without that person's permission. If Griselda is bringing *in* news that isn't hers to share, people will wonder what she's taking *out*. What's the solution?

What's It Mean?

Gossip: *Trivial verbal or written communication divulging personal, sometimes intimate, information about someone else, in either rumors or facts. Gossip can be innocent or malicious.*

1. **Pray for her.** You need to begin praying as soon as you hear that someone is gossiping or when you notice Griselda bringing inappropriate information into the group. Pray for wisdom in dealing with her and the group. Depending on her attitude, this can be a minor bump or a huge mountain in the development of trust in the group.

2. **Clarify the ground rules.** As soon as you learn about the first breach of confidentiality, remind group members how they are expected to handle anything said in the group. Go over the rules of confidentiality again. For example, say, "Let's remember that none of us has the right to share information we hear in the group, even as a prayer request. Anything someone discloses belongs to that person alone."

"I maintain that, if everyone knew what others said about him, there would not be four friends in the world." —Blaise Pascal

If you've signed a group covenant, remind members of the confidentiality clause. Take time to point out some of the Scriptural admonitions to tame the tongue, such as James 3:2-12; Proverbs 11:13; 16:28; 20:19; and 2 Corinthians 12:20. It probably isn't necessary to name any names at this point, unless the gossip has already started a wildfire. Give Griselda the benefit of the doubt—once.

WISE WORDS

"The tongue is the measure of the spiritual life of the man... [I]f we are truly mature and under the control of God, then our tongues will reveal that fact. When God has bridled the entire life, then the tongue is bridled. Thus, when the tongue is bridled it is an indicator of the measure of Lordship Christ is exercising in our members." [1]

—David H. Roper, *The Law That Sets You Free*

It may be difficult for your group members to even understand what gossip is and why it's wrong, despite strong biblical admonitions against it. The Social Issues Research Centre of Oxford, England, claims that gossip accounts for 55% of male conversation time and 67% of female conversation time. [2] No wonder gossip is so prevalent in the Christian community—everybody is doing it! And many secular researchers suggest that gossip is good and healthy, or at worst, part of the social fabric. It's no surprise, then, that many Christians think that they can share every little tidbit as a prayer request without betraying a confidence; that wrapping it as a prayer request somehow removes it from the realm of gossip. The issue of gossip needs to be clarified early and often, but realize you're trying to change a cultural norm, so be patient but firm.

3. Firmly intercept the gossip at the earliest possible point.

If the indirect approach doesn't work—and it may not—be more assertive in stopping Griselda's wagging tongue. Begin gently, but increase the firmness until she catches on. You may want to find a time you can meet privately with her. This way you can be more direct. "Griselda, I know you don't mean to hurt people by sharing their prayer needs. In fact, you probably feel like you're helping them. But you simply must not disclose any information you hear in this group. If this continues, you won't be able to stay in the group."

Tell her of any specific instances of gossip you're aware of and, if there's even the slightest doubt that you've heard the whole story, try to verify the truth. Remind Griselda that gossip, even with the best of intentions and despite the fact that everyone seems to do it, is wrong. Give her an opportunity to repent. If she refuses to acknowledge her sin, you'll need to proceed with the next step.

REMEMBER:
Gossip will destroy the life of your group faster than almost any other behavior.

4. Apply Matthew 18 to the situation.

If Griselda doesn't accept that gossip is wrong, apply Matthew 18:15-17. Take your co-leader or a person in authority in the church or organization and meet with Griselda. After praying for wisdom, approach her with an attitude of love and respect. Tell her that you are coming in the spirit of Matthew 18. Read the passage to her. You can try to understand why she's so unwilling to stop gossiping, but in the end she needs to agree that this sin needs to be dealt with like any other sin—especially since it so seriously impacts the group dynamics.

5. Ask her to leave the group.

This is absolutely the last resort, and you should use it only if there has been an ongoing, serious impact on the group. But a breach of confidence can cause irreparable wounds, and you've warned Griselda of the consequences of her actions. Even at this point, restoring confidence in the safety of the group will take effort on your part. As discussed in Chapter 1, an overriding principle of group leadership is to never sacrifice the group to minister to or contend with one person. This seems harsh, and it is. In more than 30 years of leadership, I've only had to use it a couple of times. But if one person's needs, behavior, or attitude is destroying the group, I must make a choice. As much as I may want to help Griselda, I have to put the health of the group first. If possible, I'll work with her outside the group. But I can't allow her tongue to damage group effectiveness.

> If your brother sins against you, go and show him his fault, just between the two of you. If he listens to you, you have won your brother over. But if he will not listen, take one or two others along, so that 'every matter may be established by the testimony of two or three witnesses.' If he refuses to listen to them, tell it to the church; and if he refuses to listen even to the church, treat him as you would a pagan or a tax collector.
>
> —Matthew 18:15-17

If you think you need to take this step, be sure to review Chapter 1, Principle 6 (page 14) and "The Challenge of Challenging People" in Chapter 6.

It may seem that this approach makes much ado about nothing, but gossip will destroy the life of your group faster than almost any other behavior. It's important to give it proper weight.

CHARLIE CHALLENGE — THE ARGUMENTATIVE PERSON

Charlie Challenge loves a good "discussion." He doesn't see what he's doing as being argumentative; he just enjoys a lively exchange. The problem is that his aggressive nature offends or scares the other members. Sometimes he even gets personal, calling the responses of others "dumb" or "crazy," while rolling his eyes or snorting in disdain. Note that Charlie is not merely engaged in a lively, spirited discussion. People *will* get a bit excited if they're engrossed in a stimulating exchange. That's our goal as group leaders! But Charlie moves beyond lively and spirited. He's downright rude. How can you deal with someone who steps over the line from discussion to argument?

It might be useful to understand the difference between *arguing* and *argumentation*. A person who argues, especially with hostility or condescension in his tone, usually doesn't respect others in the group or their opinions. Sometimes a person like this uses arguing as a cover-up for an inability to relate on a cordial level. Sometimes a person's need to control or shape the world the way he wants it is exhibited in aggressiveness or hostility. Sometimes this habit or attitude has become such a part of the person's personality that he doesn't even realize he's raising his voice. This is especially true of those who grew up in families where shouting and arguing were the cultural or ethnic norm. They aren't even aware that their tone is offensive to others. Frequently, however, anger is a cover-up for a deeper wound. Understand-

"People generally quarrel because they cannot argue."
—G. K. Chesterton

ing the source of Charlie's anger may help you know how to deal with him.

Argumentation, on the other hand, is more like a civil debate. It's good and healthy to hold strong opinions and to be able to form arguments or points for discussion. But in argumentation, the discussion is conducted in a mutually respectful manner. There's no place in argumentation for hostility, eye rolling, or name-calling.

1. **Pray for him.** As with so many of these challenges, it's important to *take time to pray,* both for Charlie and for your wisdom in handling him. Ask the Lord to show you what might be behind Charlie's belligerence, or at least to give you the wisdom to do no harm as you deal with him.

> "A hot-tempered man stirs up strife, but he who is slow to anger appeases contention."
>
> —Proverbs 15:18, *Amplified Bible*

2. **Clarify the ground rules.** If Charlie's attitude isn't posing an immediate problem, wait until the beginning of the next meeting to clarify how group members are expected to relate to one another. This takes the heat off of Charlie and redefines the ground rules for everyone. This may be a place to introduce the concept of "I" messages and tentative language discussed in Chapter 2. These tools can be as useful for group members as for leaders, and the skills people build as they learn them will enhance their other relationships as well.

3. **Firmly stop the argument.** If the indirect approach doesn't work—and it may not—be more assertive in stopping Charlie as soon as he becomes argumentative. Begin gently, but increase the firmness until he catches on. You might begin by repeating your ground rules in a firmer manner. For example, say, "Let's remember to consider one another's feelings as we discuss this." If that doesn't stop him, next time be more direct: "Charlie, I know you feel strongly about your position, but you simply must not insult other members of the group. Can you rephrase your comment in a way that respects the opinions of others?" I'm always

reluctant to embarrass members, but sometimes there's no other choice if I'm considering the good of the group as a whole.

4. Talk privately with Charlie.

As soon as possible after confronting him in the group, speak privately with Charlie. Schedule lunch, coffee, or another time when you can have a fairly extended time with him. Let him know that his attitude is causing division among the other members. See if you can agree on some new ways for him to respond. If he seems genuinely interested in improving his behavior, meet together several times. Continue work-

ing with him as long as you see progress and a willingness to change, and as long as he doesn't adversely affect the life of the group.

5. Ask him to leave the group.
This is absolutely the last resort, but on rare occasions it's necessary. By the time you get to this point it's often a mutual decision. Again, my standard is that I won't sacrifice the group for the sake of one individual, especially if that individual won't follow commonly accepted rules of conduct. Some people are simply not at a point in their lives where they can benefit from a group, and the typical small group is seldom a place to rehabilitate such people. Don't allow them to destroy the experience for others, but do continue to minister to Charlie if possible, or find a setting where he can learn group skills.

Memo

If you feel that you need to take this step, be sure to review Chapter 1, Principle 6 (page 14) and "The Challenge of Challenging People" in Chapter 6.

In managing Charlie, you'll need to walk a fine line to discern when argumentation turns to arguing, when passion turns to rudeness. Your group's responses will help you know when to step in.

AUDREY ARROGANT— THE DOGMATIC PERSON

Audrey Arrogant is Charlie Challenge's first cousin. She's legalistic, dogmatic, and insensitive, stepping on toes with wild abandon. There's no hint of grace in her attitude. She pronounces her opinions and responses to questions with such finality that no one dares suggest an alternative. She's trademarked the term "critical spirit." In her everyday life, she's probably a competent and productive leader, and she wants to bring the same expertise into your group. How can you offer constructive criticism to the person who's always right?

1. Pray for discernment and grace. As with Charlie, your first task is to pray for wisdom and discernment. Audrey's dogmatic approach and critical spirit could be a symptom of many problems. Perhaps she grew up in a legalistic church or home. Perhaps she has never truly experienced grace. Perhaps she's covering up insecurity. Perhaps she's afraid to risk her shaky theology to the open discussion of others' opinions. It's likely that she carries wounds from childhood that express themselves in this dogmatic, critical attitude. (See "The Emotionally Unhealthy Person," in Chapter 6 for additional insights.) As you seek wisdom from the Holy Spirit, you will better know how to approach her.

It's also important to discern if her attitude is a problem for the group or simply a personality conflict that affects

Co-leader Challenge

Knowing that Audrey is in the group, be prepared to model grace and the wisdom of a different perspective.

you more than others. If she's that insensitive it's unlikely, but do deal with your own stuff before declaring that Audrey has a problem. (See Chapter 2, "Tips for the Leader.")

You may feel both frustrated and inadequate in dealing with Audrey. She'll push buttons you didn't know you had. But blend firmness with grace and watch what God will do.

2. Begin with the indirect approach.

The best way to cope with a dogmatic person is to get her to consider alternatives. Whenever possible, avoid a direct challenge to her views. If Audrey's response is off base, use questioning rather than a direct confrontation of her error. So when Audrey responds legalistically with her air of authority, don't be threatened. Smile and gently say, "That's an interesting point, Audrey. What does someone else think about…?" Call on your co-leader or another confident person if necessary. Gently try to suggest that, on many questions, several equally correct points of view could be valid.

3. Get direct if necessary.

Legalism and dogmatism are like yeast that ferments the entire group, especially when they're accompanied by a sharp tongue. If you aren't careful, someone will be hurt. So if Audrey doesn't respond to the indirect approach or if you see that she's hurting other group members, it's time to get more direct.

4. Find a time when you can talk with Audrey privately.

Affirm her as much as you can, especially for her firm stand on the essentials of the faith. Then suggest that not everything in the discussion is an essential—that perhaps

> **For the law was given through Moses; grace and truth came through Jesus Christ.**
>
> **—John 1:17**

there are a variety of possible answers to many of the questions. Suggest that she's missing out on a wonderful opportunity to learn from other group members and that they're missing out on her wisdom because her tone often causes them to stop listening before she finishes. Your goal is to find a balance of grace and truth.

Unfortunately, most of the Audreys I've known have not taken kindly to any suggestion of fallibility. I've seen groups deteriorate over insignificant issues. I've seen hurt feelings on all sides. But I've also seen grace ministered by others in some groups. And I've seen a few Audreys come back years later, grateful that we encouraged them to be more tolerant. I've seen some change their unbiblical positions and have prayed with others for release from a critical spirit or judgmental attitude. This isn't an easy problem to face. But with prayer and grace, you may be able to moderate the negative effects of Audrey.

5. As a last resort, ask her to leave the group. As discussed in Chapter 1 and other chapters, an overriding principle of group leadership is to not sacrifice the group to minister to or contend with one person. If one person's needs, behavior, or attitude is destroying the group, you must make a choice. As much as you may want to help Audrey, you have to put the health of the group above helping one person. If possible, work with her outside the group. But don't allow

As people begin to trust one another, they'll also be more receptive to correction.

her negative influence harm the others. When Audrey's attitudes or behavior jeopardize the group, she must leave.

SYDNEY SINNER—THE UN-REPENTANT PERSON

Sydney Sinner is living a life that's clearly sinful in some area. The inventory of potential sins is too long to list, but you know them, and they're affecting your group. This is among the most difficult problems to deal with because it requires excellent discernment. What's your role in the situation?

1. Pray for wisdom.

We're all sinners. If we're looking for a perfect group filled with sinless people, we'll never find it this side of Heaven. So first, pray for wisdom and discernment. Prayerfully evaluate why you believe Sydney's sin is a problem to the group. Discern if he's chosen a lifestyle of sin, as opposed to the isolated sins that we all commit.

> **WISE WORDS**
>
> "The problem with my friends is that they're all a bunch of sinners! Seriously—every last one. That's why I fit right in."[4]
>
> —Sandra D. Wilson, *Hurt People Hurt People*

> **Warning!**
>
> Prayer is a vital response to any small group challenge. But at this stage in reading the book, perhaps you're tempted to skip over this point. Don't! Each challenge is unique and entails distinct issues to take to God. I encourage you, even now, to take a moment to pray for your Sydney and your response to him or her.

> **WISE WORDS**
>
> "In our natural state, we are creatures of *joy*. People work to get back to their natural state."
>
> —James Wilder, Ph.D.

Chances are, Sydney's sin is one of *those* sins. You know, the sexual sins: adultery, fornication, homosexuality, pornography. For some reason we seem to think that God puts these sins into an entirely separate category. Before doing anything at all, seek to understand God's opinion about the sinful lifestyle you see. While it's true that sexual sins are heinous to our Lord, let's face it—there are a bunch of other sins equally as unacceptable. If we're going to address Sydney's sin, then what about the sins of every other group member? What about pride, unbelief, hypocrisy, dishonesty, anger, etc.?

2. Evaluate the action needed. The action you take will depend on why you believe Sydney's sin is a unique problem. Is he flaunting it? Is it causing others to stumble? Do you have lambs who are being compromised? Be clear on why you want to deal with Sydney's sin and not anyone else's. You can be sure that Sydney will question your motives.

> **The church must be a grace filled, shame removed, truth-valuing community.**
>
> —Gary Gaddini

Most sins can be dealt with gently and gradually during the course of the group. And, in fact, that's usually the best choice. As people begin to trust one another, they'll also be more receptive to correction. So if the sin isn't affecting the life of the group or causing someone else in the group to stumble, I prefer to keep Sydney in the group for as long as possible.

3. Offer life in a community of belonging. If Sydney leaves the group—a community where he's found a place to belong— you'll lose your opportunity to minister to him, love him, and speak biblical counsel into his life. Often the group will decide they want Sydney to stay in order to minister to him. We experienced this with a young man who was grappling with the use of pornography. We knew that our only influence on him would be in the context of a loving community, so we welcomed him and his struggle into our lives. Over time, he was able to

> **REMEMBER:**
>
> If someone leaves the group, you'll lose the opportunity to minister to him.

renounce his addiction and join a recovery group better equipped to help him. But without the encouragement to face his sin in a shame-free zone, he might never have risked the recovery group.

Have you noticed that Christians are often afraid or unwilling to live in the mess for very long? We expect things to be neat and tidy, for people to fall into alignment quickly, for them to repent and turn around and get it right—hopefully by tomorrow afternoon. In my experience, that's a fairy tale. People and situations can get real messy before they get better. But if Sydney leaves the group, he'll lose his personal sense of belonging.

So what do you do? Recognize that the need to belong, the need for joy, offers your best hope to minister restoration and healing in the midst of a mess. Most people won't leave if they truly feel loved and accepted, even with mud all over their faces.

CONSIDER THIS...

In Chapter 1 I discussed the primary need of humans to belong. Even before birth, we have a neurological need to attach to others, and that attachment, that belonging, creates joy, which is the most basic of all emotions. Joy is the basis of bonding. It's the fruit of relationship, and people are reluctant to give up a place where they have found the true joy of belonging. This is especially true when they are going through troubled times.

4. Create an environment of openness rather than hiddenness.

If you've already set the goal of maturity (see Chapter 1), then you should expect each member of your group to desire radical personal change. If you've agreed to be open, honest, and vulnerable with one another and to love one another in the mess, you'll be ready to love Sydney back to health. And chances are, he isn't the only muddy one in the group. Each of us has attitudes and behaviors that aren't pretty. And quite frankly, each of those areas is as sinful as Sydney's seemingly flagrant attitudes and behaviors. They just seem more presentable.

When Sydney sees that the group is a safe place, he has the opportunity to flourish in the environment of openness. When he realizes that he can still belong and be accepted even in his imperfection, he may be willing to risk being vulnerable. As one person in the group finds safety, it's an encouragement to the others. Soon you'll have a depth that brings transformation to every member.

5. Talk privately with Sydney. As you learn more about Sydney, find a time when you can talk privately and at length. Lovingly and gently tell him what you've heard or seen. Say something like, "Sydney, we haven't known each other for long. I've really come to admire you, but I'm concerned for you. It's come to my attention that you and Gloria have started having sexual relations. Is that true?" Be open to the possibility that your information was inaccurate, exaggerated, or another person's bitter accusation.

Give him a chance to explain, but be alert for the excuses, justification, or anger that may follow. Clarify your position biblically by pointing out appropriate passages that relate to his situation. You might discuss 1 John 3:8-10, which sets a high behavioral standard for Christians, but remember to speak to his spirit rather than just his soul. (See Chapter 1).

6. Apply Matthew 18. If Sydney refuses to change his lifestyle *and* if his sin is causing a major problem in the group, apply Matthew 18. (See the "Griselda Gossip" section, earlier in this chapter, for a discussion of the process.) As with Griselda, take another person with you to try again. This may be your co-leader, a minister, or an elder. Discuss the sin and why it's a problem for both Sydney and the group. But always do this with the goal of restoration rather than condemnation.

7. Ask Sydney to leave the group. Yes, sometimes it's necessary to remove the offender, but *only* as the very last resort, after everything else has failed, and then only if the behavior is having a negative impact on the rest of the community. If Sydney refuses to change his behavior, you may consider it necessary to ask him to leave the group. Always try to leave the door open to continue meeting privately or serve him in any way you can. Your goal is not to be right—it's to lovingly restore him.

> Brothers, if someone is caught in a sin, you who are spiritual should restore him gently. But watch yourself, or you also may be tempted.
>
> —Galatians 6:1

The most difficult situation I ever faced in this area was when as a co-leader I needed to confront the sin of the leader shortly after the beginning of a group we had planned for months. It left me in an awkward position. It was one of scariest actions I've ever had to take. Facing this sin rather than ignoring it was a living demonstration to the group that we were serious about personal holiness, growth, and maturity. It set a standard that spurred each of us to confront our own sins and weaknesses—and to grow in important ways. By bringing sin and its consequences into the open, we all benefited. Sadly, the leader chose to leave the group and continue her lifestyle of sin rather than struggle in the mess with us. But had we pretended everything was just fine, we would have compromised everything this group had committed itself to.

So far I've taught you how to deal with some pretty difficult people. But we're just getting started! In Chapter 6, you'll learn how to lead a small group with the most challenging of challenges. Hold on tight!

1. David H. Roper, *The Law That Sets You Free* (Palo Alto, CA: Word Books Publishers in cooperation with Discovery Foundation, 1977) pp. 67, 68.

2. Kate Fox, *Evolution, Alienation and Gossip: The role of mobile telecommunications in the 21st century* (Oxford, UK: Social Issues Research Center, 2001). http://www.sirc.org/publik/gossip.shtml

3. Sandra D. Wilson, *Hurt People Hurt People* (Grand Rapids: Discovery House Publishers, 2001) p. 32.

4. Wilson, p. 123.

More Challenging Challenges

6

Sometimes you think you're in over your head. And perhaps you are. But these tips will help you identify and deal with some of the more serious challenges your group may face. Yes, you can deal with even these challenging people!

DORA DISASTER— THE PERSON WITH MULTIPLE PROBLEMS

Dora Disaster tries her best to faithfully attend the group, but her three little ones always seem to be sick. And when she's there, she consumes the group with her needs. Her husband hasn't earned enough for the family to live on for months. Last week he walked out on her and the children. She doesn't know where he is. Her mother just had a heart attack, and her frail father is helpless without his wife around. Dora's youngest was just diagnosed with ADHD, and Dora's migraine headaches are back.

> *"If some people didn't have bad luck, they wouldn't have any."*
> —Familiar Proverb

You think I'm exaggerating, but I can almost guarantee you that if Dora isn't in your group now, chances are she will be eventually! Some people seem to have a monopoly on misfortune—and they need your group. The problem is, they're so needy that you may feel ill-equipped to deal with them, and everyone else feels embarrassed to share what they consider comparatively minor needs. How can you handle this touchy situation?

1. Pray for her.

It's obvious that Dora's greatest need is for prayer—constant, consistent, committed prayer. Make it your practice to pray for Dora every day.

> "I have told you these things, so that in me you may have peace. In this world you will have trouble. But take heart! I have overcome the world."
>
> —John 16:33

Encourage others in your group to do the same. Then stand back and watch God work. Dora's circumstances may not change, but I can almost guarantee you that her outlook will. And your group will grow in faith as they see God answering her needs little by little. Celebrate the big and small victories as a faith-building exercise.

2. Encourage group members to spend time with Dora.
She needs all the support you can give her. The typical response to people like Dora is to provide intense help for acute needs, and then no support as the needs become chronic, ongoing, and endless. She needs friends to stand by her, bring her meals, supply a bag of groceries, babysit sick children, and just listen—for the long term. There will be people in your group who are particularly drawn to her. Many of those will have the gifts of mercy or helps. Privately encourage them to do whatever they can to help her or just be with her. Call her during the week to check in and pray with her, and encourage other members to do the same.

3. Provide material assistance. Encourage Dora by helping out where you can, especially anonymously. One of my great joys has been to see how the people in our various Bible study groups have taken the initiative to come through for our Doras. I've seen women spontaneously organize a grocery drive where dozens of bags of food and household products mysteriously appeared one morning. I've known of several Doras finding $50 bills in their purses or $100 bills in their mailboxes. This is truly the body of Christ at work, and it will solidify your group as few other things will.

> **Obstacles are those terrifying things we see when we take our eyes off our God.**
>
> **—Anonymous**

4. Allow Dora to share first. If your group is feeling overwhelmed and members are unwilling to share what they consider more trivial needs, you need to intervene. As needy as Dora is, others also have valid needs you can't ignore. Ask Dora to give her update first. Limit her time to something reasonable by saying, "Dora, can you take five minutes and update us on how we can pray for you?" At the end of five minutes, gently interrupt and suggest that the group stop and pray for her right now. This will affirm Dora and give her the recognition that her needs require without ignoring everyone else. It will also create some space between her sharing and that of the other members, which will lend some objectivity.

After prayer, move on to other members. Give them whatever time they require. Be sure to acknowledge that in God's eyes, every need and every person is significant. Then pray for those needs.

Be sure to acknowledge that in God's eyes, every need and every person is significant.

5. Just one need. If you're short on time, if Dora has made a habit of overwhelming the group with her needs, or if she repeats the same story every week, change your practice for a week or so. Instead of being open for all prayer needs, ask, "What *one* thing can we pray about for you this week?" Give members a minute to isolate their most important need, and then share and pray accordingly. When I've done this, some members have said, "I'm fine this week. Let Dora have my request."

6. Be alert for deeper problems. Some Doras just have a run of misfortune. But often, they are people with severe emotional problems. In my experience, many people who attract such levels of trouble are those with severe wounding in the past.

People like Dora often need a level of healing that can't be accomplished in your typical small group. However, even if you can't meet her deeper needs, Dora will benefit from the love and normalcy your group can provide. And your group will grow from the experience of being the body of Christ to her.

> *"Dear friends, do not believe every spirit, but test the spirits to see whether they are from God, because many false prophets have gone out into the world."*
>
> —1 John 4:1

CLAUDE CULT— THE LAMB STEALER

Claude Cult has no interest in your Bible study—other than to lead its members astray or lure them to his cult. Yes, some cults are known for infiltrating and destroying Christian groups. Their members are often well versed in Scripture, so you may find yourself rejoicing to have such a knowledgeable person in your group. But beware. These cults may talk about Jesus, but they don't know him or serve him. They are wolves in sheep's clothing, who will devour the lambs if you aren't careful. What do you do if you find yourself in such a situation?

Pray and listen with discernment as you begin your group.

STRATEGY 1

If someone you don't know starts attending your group, pray for discernment, especially at first. Pray that if there's anything unpleasing to the Lord, he'll reveal it to you. I've been amazed at how quickly we've been able to discern a disruptive spirit in the group. Sometimes I've spotted it; other times someone else has. There's never been a consistent giveaway. But the Lord has always been faithful in showing us quickly and with certainty when we've been awake and alert.

Words of Wisdom

"What we should read is not words, but the man behind it."

—Samuel Butler

CHECK OUT THIS IMPORTANT INFORMATION!

One of the best resources I've found for getting information and testing my suspicions about possible cult members is the Spiritual Counterfeits Project in Berkeley, California (http://www.scp-inc.org/). Their access line is open to the public at no charge at (510) 540-5767. Check their website for hours of operation. This service makes available more than 6,000 files on different cults and groups around the world, as well as the experience of staff members who have come out of cults.

STRATEGY 2

Understand the times. We live in a day when anything goes. Your religion, my religion, they're all the same. Tolerance is the watchword, and we're made to feel bigoted when we question a person's beliefs or motives. But as a leader, you need to know that there are cults that actively prey on Christian churches and groups. There are cults that send women in to seduce married men and vice versa.

There are cults that are actively committed to destroying Christian churches and marriages. These people are often

---

Consider…

A friend of mine was sitting next to a woman on an airplane. When the meal was served, she declined, saying, "No thank you. I'm fasting." Delighted to be sitting next to a believer, he asked, "Oh, are you a Christian?"

"No," she replied. "I'm a Satanist. We fast and pray every Friday for the demise of Christian marriages."

See "The Emotionally Unhealthy Person" and "The Challenge of Challenging People," later in this chapter, for additional insights.

more serious about their faith than we are. Some of these groups sound Christian and are well versed in Scripture; others make no pretense about their intent. Remember that when we come up against such people, "our struggle is not against flesh and blood, but against the rulers, against the authorities, against the powers of this dark world and against the spiritual forces of evil in the heavenly realms" (Ephesians 6:12). Active cult members operate in a spiritual dimension that many Christians are unfamiliar and uncomfortable with. They will deliberately try to confuse or embarrass you. Know what you're up against.

STRATEGY 3

Clarify the motive. I'm always a little hesitant to move too quickly in this situation, but, at the same time, indecision can be lethal. Cults use a variety of *modus operandi* to attract new members. The first time I was confronted with a Claude, the extremely knowledgeable, good-looking, and charismatic infiltrator invited our members to his Bible study during his first visit to our group.

As soon as you have any indication that a person is attending your group with impure motives, confront him. If you're not convinced by his explanation, insist on meeting privately with him within a day or two. Bring along someone more knowledgeable than you—ideally, someone who understands cults and can stay out of the labyrinth of logic and hostility you're likely to be sucked into. As soon as you're confident you're dealing with a cult member, notify your members to beware and encourage them to avoid contact until the leadership can resolve any confusion.

Judy explains how this happened in her marriage. "My husband and I reached out to a woman who was new to the church. Rebecca shared several of our interests and before we knew it, she became a close friend of the family. Soon she was at every family event, playing with the kids and helping wherever she could. It was several years before I learned she had seduced my husband, and they were having an affair. Our marriage and ministry were shattered, and we're still picking up the pieces ten years later."

STRATEGY 4

Ask him to leave. This is tough but essential. Be firm and unequivocal. As a minister told our singles group the first time we faced a group of infiltrators from a cult, "Our first responsibility is to protect the lambs." Claude may tell you he really wants to learn more about Jesus. He's sure to tell you how bigoted, discriminatory, and narrowminded you are. But your first responsibility is to protect the flock God has entrusted to you, and you're better off inviting the cult member to leave.

As inclusive as you may want to be, remember not to play with fire—protect your group.

As inclusive as you want to be, when dealing with cult infiltration, you have no choice. Get rid of cult members quickly and forcefully. Don't play with fire. *Protect the lambs.*

TERRI TOXIC — THE POISONOUS PERSON

Terri Toxic seems to have it in for you, a member in your group, or one of the leaders in your church or ministry. You've seen bitterness before, but she takes hostility to a new level. It may be that Terri is suffering from a condition called transference. If so, she'll challenge every leadership skill you have and teach you some you really didn't want.

A person in transference subconsciously identifies another person, often one in leadership or authority, with someone from the past who wounded her. This is most often a childhood wound, but may also be from someone in her adult life — perhaps a boss or a pastor or

SOME SYMPTOMS OF TRANSFERENCE

✓ She may assume you're angry when you are not.

✓ She may expect you to be devoted or particularly close to her when you don't feel that way.

✓ She may expect you to feel critical when you, in fact, feel appreciation.

✓ She may assume you feel impatient when you don't feel that at all.[2]

other church leader. She experiences the trigger person in the present as though he or she were the person from the past. Because the person in transference hasn't effectively dealt with the previous wounds, she finds it almost impossible to separate those old feelings from someone in the present who reminds her in some way of the person who wounded her. She acts out her feelings on this new, unsuspecting, and usually innocent person. Others, especially the unsuspecting target, perceive her behavior as poisonous or malicious.

What are some symptoms of this dilemma? A person in transference may mistakenly attribute some of these feelings to you or someone else in the group:

What causes a person to react this way? Author and former poisonous person Valerie J. McIntyre says, "Those in transference unconsciously set up a scenario that resembles an event from the past; they then attempt to replay the painful memories in the hope for a more satisfying resolution."[4]

An excellent book that describes the process as it shows itself in the church is *Sheep in Wolves Clothing: How Unseen Need Destroys Friendship and Community and What to Do About It*, by Valerie J. McIntyre. If you notice symptoms of transference, this book is worth reading.

WISE WORDS
"When people try to function in areas that affect their untended wounds and unhealed hurts, they inevitably hurt others. Often they wound others as severely as they were hurt, and in remarkably similar ways. While most hurting is relatively mild, deeply wounded people deeply wound others."[3]

—Sandra D Wilson, *Hurt People Hurt People*

Since the childhood events are often repressed, the person in transference is as unaware as you about what's going on. It's confusing to everyone, and you'll probably come up with a dozen different ideas before you figure out the real issue. Many people think that transference happens only in the therapist's office, but, unfortunately, it happens every day in real life. While therapists are trained to use transference in the therapeutic process, you don't have a clue what to do. While your role as a leader is not to be a professional therapist, here are a few ideas that will help you deal with Terri in your small group.

1. Pray. This one is probably out of your league. You may need help, but you will need to pray for wisdom, discernment, and the right person to help you sort out what's going on. Transference is both a psychological and spiritual issue. The open, unhealed wounds are ready fodder for demonic intrusion, which will wreak havoc with Terri's life and that of any person who gets in the way, including you. Pray before each meeting to bind and silence any demon that has been given authority because of wounding, and be

McIntyre proposes three steps that are critical to Terri's healing:

> SHE MUST ACKNOWLEDGE THAT SHE HAS MISJUDGED THE OBJECT OF HER TRANSFERENCE.

> SHE MUST HUMBLY CONFESS THAT HER ATTITUDES OR ACTIONS HAVE BEEN WRONG.

> SHE MUST ADMIT THAT SHE NEEDS HELP IN IDENTIFYING AND RESOLVING THE ISSUES FROM THE PAST WHICH SPRING THE PRESENT CONFUSION. [5]

ready for a long battle that can be won only if Terri finally understands the depth of her need.

2. Clarify what you see going on.
When you begin noticing symptoms of transference, and after informing yourself of the dynamics, broach the subject with Terri. Sometimes simply having transference explained will offer her an understanding that she has lacked. In that case, she may be willing to address the issue biblically and seek healing. Hopefully she'll at least be willing to reflect with you about what's going on.

3. Help Terri find healing for her past hurts.
God didn't bring Terri to your group to test your leadership skills or make your life miserable. He brought her to your group to offer her a chance to heal. You may have the wonderful opportunity to love her enough that she can begin to separate the past from the present and begin her healing process.

> See "Grlselda Gossip" in Chapter 5 for a more complete discussion of applying Matthew 18.

4. Apply Matthew 18 to the situation.
Terri will more likely deny the transference and find a dozen reasons to continue blaming the other person. If you are that other person, it adds complications, and you may need to bring in someone she respects to mediate.

But whether the object is you or someone else, her behavior needs to be confronted as sin. Of course, this may be complicated by the fact that she's already decided you're out to get her.

Schedule a time you can talk at length with Terri and bring someone else with you. Try again to explain what you see and how it's affecting unity within the group and in the body of Christ. Insist that she must either address the issue—usually through repentance and healing—or leave the group.

If you think you need to take this step, be sure to review Chapter 1, Principle 6 (page 14), and *"The Challenge of Challenging People"* later in this chapter.

5. Ask her to leave the group. As always, this is your last resort and should only be done prayerfully and with wise counsel. However, if Terri is unwilling to face her sin, and if her transference is causing a problem within the group, then she must leave for the good of the group. You'll want to continue working with her if at all possible, or if you're the object of the transference, find someone else who will walk beside her as she heals.

If Terri is in your group, you may think you're going crazy. Take heart. You aren't! By understanding transference, you'll have a much better chance to help her grow and mature in Christ.

Remember: God often brings people to your group to offer them a chance to heal.

TRAVIS TROUBLED— THE EMOTIONALLY UNHEALTHY PERSON

Travis Troubled doesn't quite fit in. It took you awhile to figure it out, but he really does have a serious emotional or psychological difficulty. He may be depressed or suicidal. He may think everyone is out to get him, or he may see or hear things that no one else does. He may seem like two or more different people at different times. You thought he was just odd or socially immature, but now you wonder if Travis may suffer from a mood or personality disorder. The challenge for you is that his problem is manifesting itself in ways that are disrupting the group.

> **For God has not given us a spirit of fear, but of power and of love and of a sound mind.**
> —2 Timothy 1:7, *New King James Version*

Unfortunately, untreated mental health problems seem to have increased over the past thirty years. Perhaps there actually are more of them. Perhaps we're just more aware. When I began leading groups, such problems were the exception. Now it's common to have one or more in almost every group. And sadly, many churches have done an astonishingly poor job of meeting the needs of these people. It's easier to stigmatize and ostracize than to understand and serve. Of all the problems in this book, this is probably the most difficult for most small group leaders to deal with. So what do you do?

TIP 1

Pray for wisdom and insight. Initially, you probably identified Travis's problem as something else—perhaps as one or more of the other challenges in this book. You've already tried the tips in that section and you're still baffled. Continue to pray for wisdom in handling him.

One of the first questions that will arise is whether Travis's problem is psychological or spiritual. How you answer that question will be largely based on your beliefs and the beliefs of your church. Some churches paint every problem as psychological and believe that therapy is the only solution. Others believe that psychology is of the devil and approach every problem as spiritual. I've seen both approaches heal and both approaches harm. The answer is often a balance, coupled with discernment. I encourage you to step outside your comfort zone for this challenge and consider both options.

"And God is able to make all grace abound to you, so that in all things at all times, having all that you need, you will abound in every good work."

—2 Corinthians 9:8

TIP 2

Believe that God is able, even if you aren't. When you encounter a person exhibiting these more serious challenges, you may feel totally inadequate to deal with them. You're not trained and frankly, you don't want to be. All you wanted to do was lead a small group. Let me encourage you, however, that being willing to step into this world of hurting people will result in greater rewards than anything you can imagine. How deeply you delve into it will depend on God's unique call on your life. But know that if he calls you, he will also equip you and sustain you with all the grace you need to serve Travis. Whatever you do, don't panic.

Consider the source. These profoundly wounded people may act out in a variety of ways. They may be people with depression, narcissism, dissociation, or bipolar disorder. They may be addicted to drugs, alcohol, sex, or any number of other dependencies. They may have eating disorders.

While emotional and mental problems have many causes, one of the most common culprits is childhood abuse and the way the person's body, soul, and spirit reacted to that abuse. It may have been physical, emotional, sexual, or ritualized, but all forms of abuse are damaging, and the trauma doesn't stop when the abuse stops. The current problems may be a manifestation of a deep wound that began in childhood and may have been buried for years. It needs to be healed at the source, not the symptom.

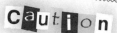

C a u t i o n

Even if you're certain that Travis is a victim of childhood abuse, don't proclaim that as a fact. You can broach it very gently as a possibility, but if he says no, leave it alone. You can still be certain that something has wounded him deeply and treat him with sensitivity and respect.

Some wounded people are aware of the details of their abuse; others will claim that they had the happiest of childhoods. But if they're exhibiting serious emotional problems, consider childhood abuse or severe wounding as at least part of the cause. Once you understand that, you'll be less critical and more willing to serve and offer a safe place for healing. (For a list of common symptoms of childhood abuse, see www.whydidntyouwarnme.com).

Don't add to their problem. Regardless of how involved God calls you to become, the most important caution is that you don't become part of the problem. Christians often do this by blaming the victim. Psychiatrist Dwight L. Carlson calls this "shooting our wounded." In our own inadequacy, we want to deflect responsibility, so we say things like, "You could change if you wanted to..." or "Why don't you just get over it?" We tell people to cheer up, calm down, step up, or sit down. We demand that they stop the addictive behavior or have more faith without realizing how condemning these words can be to a person who already feels bad about himself.

Regardless of how involved God calls you to become, be careful not to become part of the problem.

While I'm a firm believer that many mental or emotional problems can be caused by demonic intrusion or interference, you are first and foremost called to serve group members with a sacrificial love. Only then do you earn the right to intervene. One first response for many people is using healing prayer or spiritual warfare to remove demonic interference. This can be very helpful in some cases, but it can do more harm than good if performed in the absence of loving support. Dealing with an emotional problem through spiritual warfare is seldom the one-shot approach we wish it were. However, if you're trained and equipped, healing prayer in an environment of love and discipleship can bring lasting relief—in many cases, more lasting than therapy.

TIP 5

Seek professional input. Many churches have a mental health professional either on staff or in the congregation. Increasingly, pastors are trained to identify mental health problems and know when to refer to a professional. These experts are often willing to consult when those in ministry need help.

I prefer to work with licensed professionals who acknowledge the spiritual dimension in mental and emotional problems since, in my experience, an integrated approach is far more successful than one that leans exclusively to either therapy or spiritual warfare.

WISE WORDS

"Referring someone we are not competent to help is not a sign of inadequacy, weakness, or failure; rather it is a sign of genuine concern."[6]

—Stephen A. Grunlan and Daniel H. Lambrides, *Healing Relationships*

Your goal in seeking professional help is to understand Travis and what he's dealing with. When you receive this insight, you'll have a better idea of what will help him and what will make his problem even worse. Not all psychological problems can be handled in the same way. In fact, an action that may be helpful for one problem can actually be harmful for another.

TIP 6

Decide how much you can give. Ministering in healthy ways to a person like Travis can be extremely costly in terms of time and energy. While we're all called to love the wounded in our groups, not all of us are called to intensive ministry. As you begin to understand the issues, decide how much you can give. This will depend on your skills, interests, family, and other commitments—and most of all, what God is calling you to do.

The important thing here is to not commit to more than you can give. Wounded people have a tremendous sense of abandonment. They've been approached and abandoned for years. Don't add to their pain by offering to solve their every problem and then back off because it's just too much. It's better to start slowly and promise nothing than to promise unlimited help and then withdraw because the cost is too high. Most of all, be clear and communicate what you can and can't do. This is called *setting boundaries*, and it's a skill you'll need to develop.

TIP 7

Try talking with Travis. When you've considered and prayed about all of the above steps, it's time to talk to Travis. After all, you still have a group to lead and Travis's behavior is causing problems in it. Almost always, Travis knows that he has a problem. Maybe he's even under treatment or on medication. It's very possible that in the past he's been hurt by people who, in trying to help him, have instead added to his sense of guilt and condemnation.

If he sees that you really care about him as a person and aren't going to condemn him, he may be willing to work with you. If so, consider developing a signal between the two of you so you can discreetly tell him that he's "doing it again" or so he can alert you that he's feeling threatened or uncomfortable. Sometimes just having a friend who understands will be enough, particularly in the early stages of an illness.

Be sure that you avoid shaming Travis. Refer back to the discussion on guilt and shame in Chapter 2.

Of course, you also run the risk that Travis will deny that he has a problem. That's a much tougher issue and will probably require professional assistance.

TIP 8

Spend a few minutes privately with Travis before each meeting. If possible, ask Travis to arrive a few minutes before the scheduled meeting time so you can work together to address potential issues in advance rather than having them surface in the group. Check in and see how he's doing. Consider this a time to help Travis reach his goals. If you can develop a strong personal relationship with him, you'll gain credibility in his eyes. His pleasure with your attention may result in your having enough influence in his life that you can work effectively with him. Be prepared, however, for the real possibility that Travis will arrive late or not at all.

✔ **CHECK THIS OUT!**

See Chapter 1, Principal 5 on page 13 for a discussion about speaking to the spirit rather than the soul.

Look Travis in the eye and say something like, "Travis, I believe you can make it all the way through the study today." Or "Travis, the truth is, no one is trying to confuse you. If you're feeling confused, why don't we talk about it after the group time."

If he's expressing something that isn't true, it may be important to address the untruth. For example, if he's under the impression that he needs to do something disruptive, address that by speaking truth to him: "Travis, I know you may feel that you need to yell at Tony, but the truth is that yelling is not appropriate here. I need you to stop screaming, calm down, and listen so that we can continue our group."

You don't even need to quote a Bible verse. Simply look him in the eye and speak truth—gently, firmly, and often.

When you set limits, state the desired behavior first so that the recipient will hear the positive behavior before the negative or the consequence. You could say, "Travis, I need you to give other people a chance to speak right now." When possible, present limits as a choice: "Travis, you can allow others to speak or I'll have to ask you to leave the group for today. The choice is yours. We'd prefer to have you stay, but we need you to allow others a chance to speak." At this point some Travises will voluntarily leave your group; others will agree to give it a try with the new rules.

Depending on your conversations with your ministers or other professionals, you should decide just what you can and can't accept in the group. If Travis isn't already getting professional and spiritual help, ask if he's interested. If necessary, help him identify possible resources and funds. Then encourage him to make the initial calls and appointments. If he's apprehensive, you might offer to go with him the first time to help soothe his fears or shyness.

TIP 11

Remember that you are not the Messiah. It's easy to get sucked into Travis's world or to believe that you're *the one* who will help him, restore him, change him, heal him. That's called a Messiah complex, and we're all vulnerable to it to some degree. At times like this, remember that God already sent the Messiah, who has completed his redemptive and healing work on the cross. You are not called to die for Travis. You are not called to sacrifice your family for Travis. If God has a role for you in Travis's life, it will not be as his savior and it will not consume you. Remember that the Messiah's yoke is easy and his burden is light.

If you feel you can handle it, offer to continue meeting privately. If not, urge him to seek professional help and give him several telephone numbers. Follow up even after he leaves. It's especially important in this case to not let him feel abandoned. Don't just leave him to flounder unless that's his choice.

Dealing with a person suffering from mental or emotional difficulties will test your patience and skills as a leader. But it will also help you to become a more effective part of the body of Christ as you minister love, compassion, and acceptance to the troubled person. Go ahead. Step out of your comfort zone and see what God will do!

Jesus looked at them and said, 'With man this is impossible, but with God all things are possible.'
—Matthew 19:26

THE CHALLENGE OF CHALLENGING PEOPLE

For most people, leading a group with one or two challenging people is more than they bargained for. But as you gain skills and become more comfortable dealing with the challenges presented in this book, you might consider leading a group of people who don't seem to fit anywhere else. I first tried this because of my personal ministry to women who have been profoundly abused.

As mentioned in Chapter 1, many people who have suffered abuse, neglect, or other challenges growing up often find it difficult to fit into a small group. They lack both the interpersonal and group skills necessary for success. Yet, who more than these wounded ones can benefit from the ministry of a small group? Just remember, a group can either heal or harm, depending on the skill and sensitivity of the leader.

For example, one woman I discipled was invited *not* to join a recovery group she had signed up for. I'm not surprised. She's a challenge! But the rejection only added to her sense of worthlessness. What could the leader have done to include her? As I've led groups of severely wounded women, I've learned several keys about what works and what doesn't.

See the Appendix for a sample group covenant or download it from www.whydidntyouwarnme.com. Feel free to adapt this to your needs.

➤ *Be sure you have a co-leader.* While I always prefer to have a co-leader, with a group of challenging people, it's essential. You'll need the expertise of another skilled person, and it's important to have someone who can report truth to church leadership or others, should that ever be necessary.

➤ *Be clear and open when inviting participants.* Many wounded people already have had problems being part of a group, whether Christian or secular. They already feel ostracized. So I'm pretty open when I choose to lead a group of challenging people. I let them know that, in addition to Bible study, we'll be developing good group skills. Most people are eager for this.

➤ *Keep it small.* A skilled leader might be able to lead a group of six to ten members, but when dealing with challenging people, limit it to four. It's OK. It'll feel like ten! You want plenty of time to do the study and to process group issues. Plus, you can expect countless distractions that will reduce your effectiveness.

➤ *Agree to the rules in advance.* I like to use a group covenant that members read, discuss, and sign. This covenant includes meeting time, attendance and punctuality expectations, goals, confidentiality requirements, boundaries, limitations on discussion, and anything else you expect to be an issue. Members need to clearly understand your expectations and also share theirs. However, I tend to be a bit more assertive in groups like this.

> **Stress attendance and punctuality.** It's important to be clear about your expectations for both attendance and punctuality. Challenging people always have something come up. Their car breaks down, their kids get sick, they get sick, their favorite TV program is on, etc. They need to understand that their absence creates a hole in the group. They also need to understand that arriving late or leaving early is disruptive. Start on time, regardless of who is there and try very hard to end on time, regardless of how much is left to cover. Sometimes it's helpful to schedule the first 15 to 20 minutes for visiting, but clarify when members are expected to arrive and when the study or worship will begin. Talk about attendance and punctuality often and affirm those who improve in their consistency.

In one group of ten challenging people I co-led several years ago (before I had the experience to know that ten was a legion), we had a covenant for attendance. In ten weeks we had only one absence! When that one person missed a meeting, everyone else saw how important each was to the group dynamics. With only four people in the group, attendance is even more critical. While encouraging people to attend consistently and arrive on time, be realistic and learn to flex. This group will probably have a lot of attendance and punctuality issues.

> **Discuss group processes.** In a group of challenging people, some will talk all the time and others won't open their mouths. It's important to discuss expectations in advance, and then provide reminders when necessary. Model group processes by being lovingly open with both the talkers and observers. Feel free to cut off the person who never takes a breath and to call on the one who never ventures a comment. Use humor while being frank. You might even use a minute timer and agree in advance that each comment will go no longer than the time allowed. It's OK to call "time!" Praise the quiet one for speaking longer than the last time.

This may be the most difficult leadership skill of all. Challenging people are usually lonely and when they have someone to listen, many will go on and on—and on. It takes grace to lovingly cut off a member over and over—and over without discounting her contribution. But in the end, she'll be grateful.

➤ **Set personal boundaries.** Since many challenging people are lonely, they may want to become your new best friends. I set moderately firm boundaries, especially in dealing with such people. I tell members that I'm not always available to answer the telephone and that when I do, I may not be able to talk for long. I make sure members understand that my family is my priority and requires much of my time. Then if I'm spending time with family, I let the machine answer the phone, and I call back when I can. If I have limited time to talk, I tell the caller immediately, and then try to stick to that limit. Challenging people always have a crisis. They always need to talk. I need to give up my Messiah complex and remember that they reached their present age without me and will probably live many more years without my undivided attention.

➤ **Enforce confidentiality.** As with any group, confidentiality is essential. You'll hear amazing stories that you'll be tempted to share with family and friends. Don't. Even challenging people need to know their private lives are private. Enforce confidentiality in the group as well, dealing with breeches immediately and firmly. However, be aware of your state's mandated reporting requirements and follow those. Use good judgment if you learn or sense that a member or another person is being hurt or is in danger. If you have a co-leader, schedule a few minutes after the meeting to debrief before returning home. This will help you refocus and carry less emotional contamination to your family. If your group is especially challenging, you may also want to have a therapist or pastor to debrief with occasionally. Of course, these must be people who can hold a confidence.

Leading a group of challenging people can be, well—challenging. But you'll be glad you did. Watching them grow will be the most enriching experience you've had in a long time!

1. Valerie J McIntyre, *Sheep in Wolves' Clothing: How Unseen Need Destroys Friendship and Community and What to Do About It* (Grand Rapids: Baker Books, 1996, 1999) p. 13.

2. Frank Lake, *Clinical Theology: A Theological and Psychiatric Basis to Clinical Pastoral Care* (London: Darton, Longman & Todd, 1966) quoted in McIntyre, p. 36.

3. Sandra D. Wilson, *Hurt People Hurt People* (Grand Rapids: Discovery House, 2001) p. 10.

4. McIntyre, p. 43.

5. McIntyre, pp. 115, 116.

6. Stephen A. Grunlan and Daniel H. Lambrides, *Healing Relationships* (Camp Hill, PA: Christian Publications, Inc., 1984) p. 203

The End— & the Beginning

I hope that through this book you've gained a vision for the potential of small groups as an essential element of the body of Christ and the confidence to face the inevitable challenges with faith and even expectancy. In my opinion, there are few things more exciting than watching God work in the life of a challenging person, one who has experienced little success in his or her life.

You now have the tools to successfully lead almost any group and to be a catalyst for change for the wounded. Add a little common sense to the tips in this book, and you'll find new joys in leading as you watch person after person grow, change, and mature in Christ. Soon you'll have as many stories as I have, along with the joy of knowing that you made a difference in someone's life.

Be sure to check out my website at *http://www.whydidntyouwarnme.com* where new information will be posted regularly. You'll also find a link there to e-mail your success stories or questions.

HELPFUL RESOURCES

- Bramson, Robert M. *Coping with Difficult People.* Garden City, NY: Anchor Press/Doubleday, 1981.

- Carlson, Dwight L. *Why Do Christians Shoot Their Wounded? Helping (Not Hurting) Those with Emotional Difficulties.* Downers Grove, IL: InterVarsity Press, 1994.

- Fox, Kate. *Evolution, Alienation and Gossip: The role of mobile telecommunications in the 21st century.* Oxford, UK: Social Issues Research Centre, 2001. http://www.sirc.org/publik/gossip.shtml

[a] Friesen, James G. E., James Wilder, Anne M. Bierling, and Maribeth Poole, *Living from the Heart Jesus Gave You: The Essentials of Christian Living.* Van Nuys, CA: Shepherd's House, Inc., 1999.

- Gaede, S. D. *Belonging: Our Need for Community in Church and Family.* Grand Rapids: Zondervan Publishing House, 1985.

- Grunlan, Stephen A. and Daniel H. Lambrides. *Healing Relationships.* Camp Hill, PA: Christian Publications, Inc., 1984.

- Lake, Frank. *Clinical Theology: A Theological and Psychiatric Basis to Clinical Pastoral Care.* London: Darton, Longman & Todd, 1966.

- MacNutt, Francis. *Healing.* Notre Dame, IN: Ave Maria Press, 1974.

- McIntyre, Valerie J. *Sheep in Wolves' Clothing: How Unseen Need Destroys Friendship and Community and What to Do About It.* Grand Rapids: Baker Books, 1996, 1999.

- Ortberg, John. *Everybody's Normal Till You Get to Know Them.* Grand Rapids: Zondervan Publishers, 2003.

- Phipps, Robert, *Body Language Training: Shedding Light on Body Language.* http://www.bodylanguagetraining.com/

- Roper, David H. *The Law That Sets You Free.* Palo Alto, CA: Word Books Publishers in cooperation with Discovery Foundation, 1977.

- Small Group Network (http://smallgroups.com): A membership site with an abundance of information about leading small groups.

- Sweeten, Dr. Gary R. with Craig Fendley, M. Ed., *Apples of Gold: Developing the Fruit of the Spirit for Life and Ministry,* Christian Information Committee, Inc. (now Equipping Ministries International), Cincinnati, OH. Copyright © 1983.

- Wilson, Sandra D., Ph.D. *Hurt People Hurt People,* Discovery House Publishers, Grand Rapids, MI. Copyright © 2001.

SMALL GROUP COVENANT

Group Leader: _____

Phone #: _____

Group Co-leader: _____

Phone #: _____

Our Group exists to bring each member to spiritual maturity through...

SCRIPTURE: *Each member will grow in knowledge and application of the Word of God.*

WORSHIP: *Each member and the group will bring joy to God through praise, thanksgiving, and prayer.*

RELATIONSHIPS: *Each member will develop deep and lasting personal relationships in an atmosphere of acceptance and accountability.*

MINISTRY: *Each member will use his or her spiritual gifts to build up the body of Christ.*

To accomplish these goals, we mutually expect from one another:

ATTENDANCE

1) We will meet together <frequency> on <day of week>.

2) Our commitment to this group will last from <begin date> to <end date>.

3) Our meetings will begin promptly at <begin time> and close no later than <end time>.

4) We agree to be faithful in attendance and to call <name of leader or co-leader> if we cannot attend.

SCRIPTURE

1) We will study <name of study or book> and will complete the study guides to the best of our ability.

2) We agree to participate in the discussions to share what we have learned in our study and to gain from the insights of others.

3) During the meetings, the study portion will last approximately <how long>.

WORSHIP

1) The primary way(s) our group will express worship to God is <name one or more ways>.

2) We agree that our worship time will last approximately <how long>

MISSION

1) The primary purpose of our group is <identify>.

2) We will seek to take part in ministry as a group through <name service project, other>.

3) We will develop, encourage, and use our spiritual gifts within the group by <insert ways> and outside the group by <insert ways>.

COMMUNITY, TRANSPARENCY, AND ACCOUNTABILITY

1) Is our group open to having new members join? Yes __ No __

2) The primary ways our group will seek to build openness and accountability are: <insert ways>.

3) The amount of time given for sharing or disclosure at each meeting will be approximately <how long>.

4) Refreshments will be handled by <define>.

5) We will have time for informal conversation before the meeting for <how long> or after meeting for <how long>.

PRAYER

1) The amount of time devoted to prayer within the group will be approximately <how long>.

2) Prayer in the group setting <will/will not> be limited to specific needs. If so, <define >.

OTHER

1) Children over/under the age of <specify> <will/will not> attend the meetings.

2) How will childcare be handled? <specify>

3) At the end of our group commitment, we will complete an evaluation. <Yes/No>.

I agree to do my best to honor this group covenant.

Member's signature: _____ _____ _____

CHECK OUT THIS VAUABLE COUPON!

FREE

SMALL GROUP RESOURCES

For MORE HELP, check out the small group leader resources on *SmallGroups.com*.

With the purchase of this book, you are entitled to a free one-month membership at *www.SmallGroups.com*. To claim your **FREE** membership:

- ➤ Go to: *www.SmallGroups.com/freemembership*.
- ➤ Continue through "checkout" process.
- ➤ Select payment method "check/money order." However, no payment is due if you use coupon code: **stdsg06**
- ➤ Then click "Redeem" and "Confirm Order" for your free membership!

Redeem your coupon *today!*